Favorite Brand Name™
Diabetic Recipes

Publications International, Ltd.

Publications International, Ltd.

snacks
contents

dipped & spread

Garlic Bean Dip

4 cloves garlic
1 can (about 15 ounces) pinto or black beans, rinsed
   and drained
¼ cup pimiento-stuffed green olives
4½ teaspoons lemon juice
½ teaspoon ground cumin
   Assorted fresh vegetables and crackers (optional)

1. Place garlic in food processor; process until minced. Add beans, olives, lemon juice and cumin; process until well blended but not entirely smooth.

2. Serve with vegetables and crackers.

Makes 12 servings (about 1½ cups)

Note: Cumin is a widely used spice in Middle Eastern, Asian and Mediterranean cooking. It is available in seed and ground form and adds a nutty flavor to dishes.

Hint: Buy fresh vegetables, such as carrots, celery and red bell peppers, already cut up from the produce section of the supermarket.

Prep Time: 10 minutes

Nutrients per Serving (2 tablespoons dip [without vegetables and crackers]):
Calories: 42, **Calories from Fat:** 21%, **Total Fat:** 1g,
Saturated Fat: <1g, **Cholesterol:** 0mg, **Sodium:** 207mg,
Carbohydrate: 7g, **Dietary Fiber:** 1g, **Protein:** 3g

Dietary Exchanges: ½ Starch

Nutty Carrot Spread

¼ **cup finely chopped pecans**

6 **ounces cream cheese, softened**

2 **tablespoons frozen orange juice concentrate,
thawed**

¼ **teaspoon ground cinnamon**

1 **cup shredded carrots**

¼ **cup raisins**

36 **toasted slices party pumpernickel bread or melba
toast rounds**

1. Preheat oven to 350°F. Place pecans on shallow baking pan. Bake 6 to 8 minutes or until lightly toasted, stirring occasionally. Cool slightly.

2. Meanwhile, combine cream cheese, juice concentrate and cinnamon in small bowl; stir until well blended. Stir in carrots, pecans and raisins.

3. Serve spread with bread or crackers.   *Makes 18 servings*

Nutrients per Serving (2 bread slices with about 2 tablespoons cream cheese mixture [about 1 tablespoon per slice]):
Calories: 68, **Calories from Fat:** 19%, **Total Fat:** 1g,
Saturated Fat: <1g, **Cholesterol:** 2mg, **Sodium:** 149mg,
Carbohydrate: 11g, **Dietary Fiber:** <1g, **Protein:** 3g

Dietary Exchanges: ½ Starch, ½ Fat

Nutty Carrot Spread

Asian Peanut Butter Dip

> 3 tablespoons reduced-fat creamy peanut butter
> 2 tablespoons apple butter
> 2 tablespoons fat-free (skim) milk
> 1 tablespoon reduced-sodium soy sauce
> 1½ teaspoons lime juice
> 10 stalks celery, cut into fourths

Combine peanut butter, apple butter, milk, soy sauce and lime juice in small bowl; whisk together until very smooth. Store, tightly sealed, in refrigerator. Serve with celery.

Makes 5 servings

Travel Tip: Divide dip among five individual plastic containers; cover tightly. Divide celery among five small resealable food storage bags. Store in cooler with ice.

Nutrients per Serving (2 tablespoons dip with 8 celery pieces):
Calories: 70, **Calories from Fat:** 21%, **Total Fat:** 3g,
Saturated Fat: <1g, **Cholesterol:** <1mg, **Sodium:** 218mg,
Carbohydrate: 10g, **Dietary Fiber:** 2g, **Protein:** 3g

Dietary Exchanges: ½ Fruit, 1 Vegetable, ½ Fat

> tip
>
> Apple butter is a richly flavored preserve made by slowly cooking apples, apple cider, sugar and spices together over low heat. It can be found with jams, jellies and honeys in most large supermarkets.

Asian Peanut Butter Dip

Seafood Spread

1 package (8 ounces) cream cheese, softened
½ pound smoked whitefish, skinned, boned and flaked
2 tablespoons minced green onion
1 tablespoon plus 1 teaspoon chopped fresh dill
1 teaspoon lemon juice
¼ teaspoon black pepper
   Rye bread halves (optional)
   Lime wedges (optional)

1. Beat cream cheese in medium bowl with electric mixer at medium speed until smooth. Add whitefish, green onion, dill, lemon juice and pepper; mix until well blended. Refrigerate until ready to serve.

2. Serve with rye bread slices, if desired, and garnish with lime wedges. *Makes 12 servings (1½ cups)*

Prep Time: 10 minutes

Nutrients per Serving (2 tablespoons spread [without bread]):
Calories: 87, **Calories from Fat:** 70%, **Total Fat:** 7g,
Saturated Fat: 4g, **Cholesterol:** 27mg, **Sodium:** 249mg,
Carbohydrate: 1g, **Dietary Fiber:** <1g, **Protein:** 6g

Dietary Exchanges: 1 Lean Meat, 1 Fat

Seafood Spread

Bacon & Cheese Dip

2 packages (8 ounces each) reduced-fat cream
    cheese, softened and cut into cubes
4 cups (16 ounces) shredded reduced-fat sharp
    Cheddar cheese
1 cup evaporated fat-free (skim) milk
2 tablespoons yellow mustard
1 tablespoon chopped onion
2 teaspoons Worcestershire sauce
½ teaspoon salt
¼ teaspoon hot pepper sauce (optional)
1 pound turkey bacon, crisp-cooked and crumbled
    Vegetable dippers or crusty bread (optional)

SLOW COOKER DIRECTIONS

1. Place cream cheese, Cheddar cheese, evaporated milk, mustard, onion, Worcestershire sauce, salt and hot pepper sauce, if desired, in slow cooker. Cover; cook on LOW, stirring occasionally, 1 hour or until cheese melts.

2. Stir in bacon; adjust seasonings as desired. Serve with vegetable dippers or crusty bread.

Makes 32 servings (about 4 cups dip)

Nutrients per Serving (2 tablespoons dip [without vegetables or bread]):
Calories: 114, **Calories from Fat:** 64%, **Total Fat:** 8g,
Saturated Fat: 4g, **Cholesterol:** 27mg, **Sodium:** 436mg,
Carbohydrate: 2g, **Dietary Fiber:** <1g, **Protein:** 7g

Dietary Exchanges: 1 Lean Meat, 1 Fat

Chunky Hawaiian Spread

**1 can (8 ounces) DOLE® Crushed Pineapple, well
   drained**
½ cup fat free or light sour cream
1 package (3 ounces) light cream cheese, softened
¼ cup mango chutney*
Low fat crackers

*If there are large pieces of fruit in chutney, cut them into small pieces.

• Beat crushed pineapple, sour cream, cream cheese and chutney in bowl until blended. Cover and chill 1 hour or overnight. Serve with crackers. Refrigerate any leftover spread in airtight container for up to one week.

Makes 2½ cups spread

Nutrients per Serving (2 tablespoons spread [without crackers]):
Calories: 28, **Calories from Fat:** 22%, **Total Fat:** 1g,
Saturated Fat: <1g, **Cholesterol:** 2mg, **Sodium:** 33mg,
Carbohydrate: 5g, **Dietary Fiber:** <1g, **Protein:** 1g

Dietary Exchanges: ½ Fruit

---

tip

Mango chutney is a tasty condiment popular in Indian cooking. A blend of mango, vinegar, sugar and spices, it adds a unique flavor to any dish. Chutneys are often located in the ethnic foods section of the supermarket.

Chunky Hawaiian Spread

Fast Guacamole and "Chips"

 2 ripe avocados
½ cup chunky salsa
¼ teaspoon hot pepper sauce (optional)
½ seedless cucumber, sliced into ⅛-inch-thick rounds

1. Cut avocados in half; remove and discard pits. Scoop flesh into medium bowl; mash with fork.

2. Add salsa and hot pepper sauce, if desired; mix well.

3. Transfer guacamole to serving bowl. Serve with cucumber "chips." *Makes 8 servings*

Nutrients per Serving (about 3½ tablespoons guacamole with cucumber chips):
Calories: 85, **Calories from Fat:** 72%, **Total Fat:** 7g,
Saturated Fat: 1g, **Cholesterol:** 0mg, **Sodium:** 120mg,
Carbohydrate: 5g, **Dietary Fiber:** 2g, **Protein:** 2g

Dietary Exchanges: 1 Vegetable, 1½ Fat

Fast Guacamole and "Chips"

Fresh Fruit with Creamy Lime Dipping Sauce

1 small jicama, peeled and cut into ½-inch-thick strips 3 to 4 inches long
2 tablespoons lime juice
2 pounds watermelon, rind removed, cut into ½-inch-thick wedges 2 to 3 inches wide
½ small pineapple, rind removed, halved lengthwise and cut crosswise into wedges
1 ripe papaya, peeled, seeded and sliced crosswise
Creamy Lime Dipping Sauce (recipe follows)

Combine jicama and lime juice in large bowl; toss. Drain. Arrange jicama, watermelon, pineapple and papaya on large platter. Serve with Creamy Lime Dipping Sauce.

Makes 12 servings

Creamy Lime Dipping Sauce

1 container (6 ounces) vanilla fat-free yogurt
2 tablespoons minced fresh cilantro
2 tablespoons lime juice
1 tablespoon minced jalapeño pepper*

*Jalapeño peppers can sting and irritate the skin, so wear rubber gloves when handling peppers and do not touch your eyes.

Combine all ingredients in small bowl; mix well to combine.

Makes about 1 cup

Nutrients per Serving (¹⁄₁₂ of total recipe):
Calories: 65, **Calories from Fat:** 5%, **Total Fat:** <1g,
Saturated Fat: 0g, **Cholesterol:** <1mg, **Sodium:** 23mg,
Carbohydrate: 15g, **Dietary Fiber:** 1g, **Protein:** 1g

Dietary Exchanges: 1 Fruit

Asian Salsa and
Easy Wonton Chips

  1 cup diced unpeeled cucumber
½ cup thinly sliced green onions
½ cup chopped red bell pepper
⅓ cup coarsely chopped fresh cilantro
  2 tablespoons reduced-sodium soy sauce
  1 tablespoon rice vinegar
  1 clove garlic, minced
½ teaspoon dark sesame oil
¼ teaspoon red pepper flakes
    Easy Wonton Chips (recipe follows) or assorted
      fresh vegetables for dipping

1. Combine cucumber, green onions, bell pepper, cilantro, soy sauce, rice vinegar, garlic, oil and red pepper flakes in medium bowl until well blended.

2. Cover and refrigerate until serving time. Serve with Easy Wonton Chips or assorted fresh vegetables for dipping. Or, use as an accompaniment to broiled fish, chicken or pork.

Makes 4 servings

Easy Wonton Chips

  1 tablespoon reduced-sodium soy sauce
  2 teaspoons peanut or vegetable oil
½ teaspoon sugar
¼ teaspoon garlic salt
12 wonton wrappers
    Nonstick cooking spray

1. Preheat oven to 375°F. Combine soy sauce, oil, sugar and garlic salt in small bowl; mix well.

continued on page 22

Asian Salsa and Easy Wonton Chips, continued

2. Cut each wonton wrapper diagonally in half. Place on 15×10-inch jelly-roll pan coated with nonstick cooking spray. Brush soy sauce mixture lightly over both sides of wrappers.

3. Bake 4 to 6 minutes or until crisp and lightly browned, turning after 3 minutes. Transfer to cooling rack; cool completely. *Makes 2 dozen chips*

Nutrients per Serving (¼ cup salsa with 6 Easy Wonton Chips):
Calories: 116, **Calories from Fat:** 25%, **Total Fat:** 3g,
Saturated Fat: <1g, **Cholesterol:** 2mg, **Sodium:** 723mg,
Carbohydrate: 17g, **Dietary Fiber:** 1g, **Protein:** 4g

Dietary Exchanges: 1 Starch, ½ Vegetable, ½ Fat

Herbed Yogurt Dip with Vegetables

2 cups plain fat-free or low-fat yogurt
3 tablespoons sliced green onions
1 tablespoon finely chopped fresh parsley
½ teaspoon Italian seasoning
¼ teaspoon garlic powder
3 stalks celery, cut into 10 sticks
½ medium cucumber, cut into 10 sticks

Combine yogurt, green onions, parsley, Italian seasoning and garlic powder in small bowl. Cover; refrigerate at least 2 hours. Serve with celery and cucumber sticks. *Makes 10 servings*

Prep Time: 10 minutes
Chill Time: 6 hours

Nutrients per Serving (1 tablespoon dip with 1 celery stalk and 1 cucumber stick):
Calories: 26, **Calories from Fat:** 1%, **Total Fat:** <1g,
Saturated Fat: <1g, **Cholesterol:** 1mg, **Sodium:** 41mg,
Carbohydrate: 5g, **Dietary Fiber:** 1g, **Protein:** 2g

Dietary Exchanges: Free

Olive Tapenade

        1 cup pitted black olives, drained
        ½ cup chopped fresh parsley
        ¼ cup olive oil
        1 clove garlic, minced
        1 tablespoon dried onion
        1 tablespoon chopped fresh basil
        1 tablespoon balsamic vinegar
        ⅛ teaspoon red pepper flakes
        ⅛ teaspoon hot pepper sauce
        2 tablespoons chopped pimientos
           Pita bread wedges

Combine all ingredients except pimientos and pita bread wedges in a food processor and blend until smooth. Stir in pimentos and serve with pita bread wedges.

Makes 18 servings

Favorite recipe from **Wheat Foods Council**

Nutrients per Serving (1 tablespoon tapenade [without pita wedges]):
Calories: 38, **Calories from Fat:** 88%, **Total Fat:** 4g,
Saturated Fat: <1g, **Cholesterol:** 0mg, **Sodium:** 67mg,
Carbohydrate: 1g, **Dietary Fiber:** <1g, **Protein:** <1g

Dietary Exchanges: 1 Fat

tip

If you have leftover canned olives from this recipe, transfer them to a glass jar for storage. Olives will keep for several weeks in the refrigerator. When the olives begin to turn soft, discard them.

Berry Good Dip

**8 ounces fresh strawberries or thawed frozen
    unsweetened strawberries
4 ounces fat-free cream cheese, softened
¼ cup reduced-fat sour cream
1 tablespoon sugar
    Orange peel (optional)
    Fresh fruit, such as apples, strawberries, pineapple
    and oranges**

1. Place strawberries in food processor or blender; process until smooth.

2. Beat cream cheese in small bowl until smooth. Stir in sour cream, strawberry purée and sugar; cover. Refrigerate until ready to serve.

3. Spoon dip into small serving bowl. Garnish with orange peel. Serve with assorted fresh fruit for dipping.

Makes 6 (¼-cup) servings

Cook's Tip: For a super quick fruit spread for toasted mini English muffins or bagels, beat 1 package (8 ounces) softened fat-free cream cheese in small bowl until fluffy. Stir in 3 to 4 tablespoons strawberry fruit spread. Sweeten to taste with 1 to 2 teaspoons sugar, if desired. Makes 6 servings.

Nutrients per Serving (¼ cup dip [without fruit dippers]):
Calories: 47, **Calories from Fat:** 16%, **Total Fat:** 1g,
Saturated Fat: <1g, **Cholesterol:** 7mg, **Sodium:** 120mg,
Carbohydrate: 6g, **Dietary Fiber:** 1g, **Protein:** 3g

Dietary Exchanges: ½ Fruit, ½ Lean Meat

Chutney Cheese Spread

2 packages (8 ounces each) fat-free cream cheese, softened
1 cup (4 ounces) shredded reduced-fat Cheddar cheese
½ cup mango chutney
¼ cup sliced green onions
3 tablespoons dark raisins, chopped
2 cloves garlic, minced
1 to 1½ teaspoons curry powder
¾ teaspoon ground coriander
½ to ¾ teaspoon ground ginger
1 tablespoon chopped dry-roasted peanuts

1. Place cream cheese and Cheddar cheese in food processor or blender. Cover; process until smooth. Stir in chutney, green onions, raisins, garlic, curry powder, coriander and ginger. Cover; refrigerate 2 to 3 hours.

2. Sprinkle peanuts over spread just before serving. Serve with toasted bread slices, if desired. *Makes about 20 servings*

Variation: Try substituting 1 tablespoon toasted coconut for the peanuts in this recipe to give it a slightly sweeter flavor.

Nutrients per Serving (2 tablespoons spread [without toasted bread slices]):
Calories: 58, **Calories from Fat:** 18%, **Total Fat:** 1g, **Saturated Fat:** <1g, **Cholesterol:** 7mg, **Sodium:** 218mg, **Carbohydrate:** 7g, **Dietary Fiber:** <1g, **Protein:** 5g

Dietary Exchanges: ½ Fruit, ½ Lean Meat

Fresh Tomato Eggplant Spread

1 medium eggplant
2 large ripe tomatoes, seeded and chopped
1 cup minced zucchini
¼ cup chopped green onions
2 tablespoons red wine vinegar
1 clove garlic, minced
1 tablespoon olive oil
1 tablespoon finely chopped fresh basil
2 teaspoons finely chopped fresh oregano
1 teaspoon finely chopped fresh thyme
1 teaspoon honey
⅛ teaspoon black pepper
¼ cup pine nuts or slivered almonds
32 melba toast rounds

1. Preheat oven to 375°F. Poke holes in surface of eggplant with fork. Place in shallow baking pan. Bake 20 to 25 minutes or until tender. Cool completely. Peel and discard skin; finely chop eggplant. Place in colander; press to squeeze out excess liquid.

2. Combine eggplant, tomatoes, zucchini, green onions, vinegar, garlic, oil, basil, oregano, thyme, honey and black pepper in large bowl. Mix well. Cover; refrigerate 2 hours to allow flavors to blend.

3. Stir in pine nuts just before serving. Serve with melba toast rounds. *Makes 8 servings*

Nutrients per Serving (⅛ of spread with 4 melba toast rounds):
Calories: 117, **Calories from Fat:** 31%, **Total Fat:** 4g,
Saturated Fat: 0g, **Cholesterol:** 0mg, **Sodium:** 65mg,
Carbohydrate: 15g, **Dietary Fiber:** 2g, **Protein:** 4g

Dietary Exchanges: ½ Starch, 1½ Vegetable, ½ Fat

Warm Peanut-Caramel Dip

¼ cup reduced-fat peanut butter
2 tablespoons fat-free (skim) milk
2 tablespoons fat-free caramel ice cream topping
1 large apple, thinly sliced
4 large pretzel rods, broken in half

1. Combine peanut butter, milk and caramel topping in small saucepan. Heat over low heat, stirring constantly, until mixture is melted and warm.

2. Serve with apple slices and pretzel rods.

Makes 4 servings

Microwave Directions: Combine all ingredients except apple slices and pretzel rods in small microwavable dish. Microwave on MEDIUM (50%) 1 minute; stir well. Microwave an additional minute or until mixture is melted and warm.

Nutrients per Serving (about 1½ tablespoons dip with 4 apple slices and 2 pretzel halves):
Calories: 185, **Calories from Fat:** 34%, **Total Fat:** 7g,
Saturated Fat: 1g, **Cholesterol:** <1mg, **Sodium:** 274mg,
Carbohydrate: 27g, **Dietary Fiber:** 2g, **Protein:** 6g

Dietary Exchanges: 2 Starch, 1 Fat

wrapped, rolled & skewered

Chicken Wraps

½ **pound boneless skinless chicken thighs**
½ **teaspoon Chinese 5-spice powder**
½ **cup canned bean sprouts, rinsed and drained**
2 **tablespoons sliced almonds**
2 **tablespoons minced green onion**
2 **tablespoons soy sauce**
4 **teaspoons hoisin sauce**
1 to 2 **teaspoons hot chili sauce with garlic***
4 **large leaves romaine, iceberg or bibb lettuce**

Hot chili sauce with garlic is available in the Asian foods section of most large supermarkets.

1. Preheat oven to 350°F. Place chicken thighs on baking sheet; sprinkle with 5-spice powder. Bake 20 minutes or until chicken is cooked through. Cool; dice chicken.

2. Place chicken, bean sprouts, almonds, green onion, soy sauce, hoisin sauce and chili sauce in large bowl. Stir gently until blended. To serve, spoon ⅓ cup chicken mixture onto each lettuce leaf; roll or fold as desired. *Makes 4 servings*

Nutrients per Serving (1 wrap):
Calories: 114, **Calories from Fat:** 24%, **Total Fat:** 5g, **Saturated Fat:** 1g, **Cholesterol:** 47mg, **Sodium:** 302mg, **Carbohydrate:** 5g, **Dietary Fiber:** 1g, **Protein:** 13g

Dietary Exchanges: 1 Vegetable, 1½ Lean Meat

Chicken Wrap

Greek Spinach-Cheese Rolls

1 loaf (1 pound) frozen bread dough
1 package (10 ounces) frozen chopped spinach,
   thawed and squeezed dry
¾ cup (3 ounces) crumbled feta cheese
½ cup (2 ounces) shredded reduced-fat Monterey Jack
   cheese
4 green onions, thinly sliced
1 teaspoon dried dill weed
½ teaspoon garlic powder
½ teaspoon black pepper

1. Thaw bread dough according to package directions. Spray 15 standard (2½-inch) muffin cups with nonstick cooking spray; set aside. Roll out dough on lightly floured surface to 15×9-inch rectangle. (If dough is springy and difficult to roll, cover with plastic wrap and let rest 5 minutes to relax.) Position dough so long edge is parallel to edge of work surface.

2. Combine spinach, cheeses, green onions, dill weed, garlic powder and pepper in large bowl; mix well.

3. Sprinkle spinach mixture evenly over dough to within 1 inch of long edges. Starting at long edge, roll up snugly, pinching seam closed. Place roll seam side down; cut roll with serrated knife into 15 slices. Place slices, cut sides up, in prepared muffin cups. Cover with plastic wrap; let stand 30 minutes in warm place until rolls are slightly puffy.

4. Preheat oven to 375°F. Bake 20 to 25 minutes or until golden. Serve warm or at room temperature. Rolls can be stored in refrigerator in airtight container up to 2 days.

Makes 15 rolls

Nutrients per Serving (1 roll):
Calories: 111, **Calories from Fat:** 24%, **Total Fat:** 3g,
Saturated Fat: 2g, **Cholesterol:** 8mg, **Sodium:** 267mg,
Carbohydrate: 16g, **Dietary Fiber:** <1g, **Protein:** 5g

Dietary Exchanges: 1 Starch, ½ Lean Meat

Mini Marinated Beef Skewers

1 boneless beef top sirloin steak (about 1 pound)
2 tablespoons dry sherry
2 tablespoons soy sauce
1 tablespoon dark sesame oil
2 cloves garlic, minced
18 cherry tomatoes
Lettuce leaves (optional)

1. Cut beef crosswise into ⅛-inch slices. Place in large resealable food storage bag. Combine sherry, soy sauce, sesame oil and garlic in small bowl; pour over steak. Seal bag; turn to coat. Marinate in refrigerator at least 30 minutes or up to 2 hours. Soak 18 (6-inch) wooden skewers in water 20 minutes.

2. Preheat broiler. Drain beef; discard marinade. Weave beef accordion style onto skewers. Place on rack of broiler pan.

3. Broil 4 to 5 inches from heat 4 minutes. Turn skewers over; broil 4 minutes or until beef is barely pink in center. Place one cherry tomato on each skewer; transfer to lettuce-lined platter, if desired. Serve warm or at room temperature.

Makes 18 appetizers

Nutrients per Serving (2 skewers):
Calories: 72, **Calories from Fat:** 34%, **Total Fat:** 3g,
Saturated Fat: 1g, **Cholesterol:** 19mg, **Sodium:** 169mg,
Carbohydrate: 2g, **Dietary Fiber:** <1g, **Protein:** 10g

Dietary Exchanges: 1 Lean Meat, ½ Vegetable

Peanut Pitas

> 1 package (8 ounces) small rounds pita bread, cut in half
> 16 teaspoons reduced-fat peanut butter
> 16 teaspoons strawberry fruit spread
> 1 large banana, peeled and thinly sliced (about 48 slices)

1. Spread inside of each pita half with 1 teaspoon peanut butter and 1 teaspoon fruit spread.

2. Fill pita halves evenly with banana slices. Serve immediately.

Makes 8 servings

Honey Bees: Substitute honey for fruit spread.

Jolly Jellies: Substitute any flavor jelly for fruit spread and thin apple slices for banana slices.

P. B. Crunchers: Substitute reduced-fat mayonnaise for fruit spread and celery slices for banana slices.

Nutrients per Serving (2 Peanut Pita halves):
Calories: 167, **Calories from Fat:** 24%, **Total Fat:** 5g,
Saturated Fat: 1g, **Cholesterol:** 0mg, **Sodium:** 177mg,
Carbohydrate: 26g, **Dietary Fiber:** <1g, **Protein:** 6g

Dietary Exchanges: 2 Starch, ½ Fat

Roast Beef Roll-Ups

2 tablespoons fat-free mayonnaise
½ teaspoon prepared horseradish
2 slices deli roast beef (about 1 ounce each)
6 tablespoons crumbled blue cheese
2 thin slices red onion, quartered

1. Combine mayonnaise and horseradish in small bowl; spread over 1 side of each roast beef slice.

2. Top with blue cheese and onion. Roll up each slice tightly to make two rolls. *Makes 1 serving*

Nutrients per Serving (1 roll-up):
Calories: 124, **Calories from Fat:** 51%, **Total Fat:** 7g,
Saturated Fat: 4g, **Cholesterol:** 36mg, **Sodium:** 567mg,
Carbohydrate: 4g, **Dietary Fiber:** 1g, **Protein:** 10g

Dietary Exchanges: ½ Vegetable, 1½ Lean Meat, 1 Fat

Watermelon Kebobs

18 (1-inch) cubes seedless watermelon
6 ounces (1-inch cubes) fat-free turkey breast
6 ounces (1-inch cubes) reduced-fat Cheddar cheese
6 (6-inch) bamboo skewers

Alternate cubes of watermelon between cubes of turkey and cheese threaded onto each skewer. *Makes 6 servings*

Favorite recipe from **National Watermelon Promotion Board**

Nutrients per Serving (1 kebob):
Calories: 143, **Calories from Fat:** 61%, **Total Fat:** 10g,
Saturated Fat: 6g, **Cholesterol:** 39mg, **Sodium:** 390mg,
Carbohydrate: 2g, **Dietary Fiber:** <1g, **Protein:** 12g

Dietary Exchanges: 2 Lean Meat, 1 Fat

Tortellini Teasers

Zesty Tomato Sauce (recipe follows)
½ (9-ounce) package refrigerated cheese tortellini
1 large red or green bell pepper, cut into 1-inch pieces
2 medium carrots, cut into ½-inch pieces
1 medium zucchini, cut into ½-inch pieces
12 medium mushrooms
12 cherry tomatoes

1. Prepare Zesty Tomato Sauce; keep warm.

2. Cook tortellini according to package directions; drain.

3. Alternate tortellini and 2 to 3 vegetable pieces on long toothpicks or wooden skewers. Serve as dippers with tomato sauce. *Makes 6 servings*

Zesty Tomato Sauce

1 can (15 ounces) tomato purée
2 tablespoons finely chopped onion
2 tablespoons chopped fresh parsley
1 teaspoon dried oregano
¼ teaspoon dried thyme
¼ teaspoon salt
⅛ teaspoon black pepper

Combine tomato purée, onion, parsley, oregano and thyme in small saucepan. Heat thoroughly, stirring occasionally. Stir in salt and pepper.

Nutrients per Serving (1 kabob with about ¼ cup Zesty Tomato Sauce):
Calories: 130, **Calories from Fat:** 15%, **Total Fat:** 2g,
Saturated Fat: 1g, **Cholesterol:** 12mg, **Sodium:** 306mg,
Carbohydrate: 23g, **Dietary Fiber:** 5g, **Protein:** 7g

Dietary Exchanges: 1 Starch, 2 Vegetable

Asian Vegetable Rolls with Soy-Lime Dipping Sauce

¼ **cup reduced-sodium soy sauce**
2 **tablespoons lime juice**
1 **clove garlic, crushed**
1 **teaspoon honey**
½ **teaspoon finely chopped fresh ginger**
¼ **teaspoon dark sesame oil**
⅛ **to** ¼ **teaspoon red pepper flakes**
½ **cup grated cucumber**
⅓ **cup grated carrot**
¼ **cup sliced yellow bell pepper (1 inch long)**
2 **tablespoons thinly sliced green onion**
18 **small leaf lettuce leaves or Bibb lettuce leaves from inner part of head**
Sesame seeds (optional)

1. Combine soy sauce, lime juice, garlic, honey, ginger, oil and pepper flakes in small bowl. Combine cucumber, carrot, bell pepper and green onion in medium bowl. Add 1 tablespoon soy sauce mixture to vegetable mixture; stir until blended.

2. Place about 1 tablespoon vegetable mixture on each lettuce leaf. Roll up leaves; top with sesame seeds just before serving, if desired. Serve with remaining sauce.   *Makes 6 servings*

Prep Time: 15 minutes

Nutrients per Serving (3 rolls with 1 tablespoon dipping sauce):
Calories: 25, **Calories from Fat:** 11%, **Total Fat:** <1g,
Saturated Fat: <1g, **Cholesterol:** 0mg, **Sodium:** 343mg,
Carbohydrate: 5g, **Dietary Fiber:** 1g, **Protein:** 1g

Dietary Exchanges: Free

Asian Vegetable Rolls with
Soy-Lime Dipping Sauce

Mexican Roll-Ups

6 uncooked lasagna noodles
¾ cup prepared guacamole
¾ cup chunky salsa
¾ cup (3 ounces) shredded fat-free Cheddar cheese
    Additional salsa (optional)

1. Cook lasagna noodles according to package directions, omitting salt. Rinse with cool water; drain. Cool.

2. Spread 2 tablespoons guacamole onto each noodle; top each with 2 tablespoons salsa and 2 tablespoons cheese.

3. Roll up noodles jelly-roll style. Cut each roll-up in half to form two equal-size pieces. Serve immediately with additional salsa, if desired, or cover with plastic wrap and refrigerate up to 3 hours.   *Makes 12 appetizers*

Nutrients per Serving (1 roll-up):
Calories: 77, **Calories from Fat:** 28%, **Total Fat:** 1g, **Saturated Fat:** 0g, **Cholesterol:** 2mg, **Sodium:** 218mg, **Carbohydrate:** 11g, **Dietary Fiber:** 1g, **Protein:** 3g

Dietary Exchanges: 1 Starch

tip

These quick and easy appetizers use prepared guacamole and salsa to save time, but you could easily substitute homemade guacamole and a simple Pico de Gallo to make them even more special.

Mexican Roll-Ups

Caribbean Chutney Kabobs

½ **medium pineapple**
¾ **pound boneless skinless chicken breasts, cut into**
  1-inch pieces
1 **medium red bell pepper, cut into 1-inch pieces**
20 **(4-inch) wooden skewers***
½ **cup mango chutney**
2 **tablespoons orange juice or pineapple juice**
1 **teaspoon vanilla**
¼ **teaspoon ground nutmeg**

*To prevent burning, soak skewers in water at least 20 minutes before assembling kabobs.

1. Peel and core pineapple. Cut pineapple into 1-inch chunks. Alternately thread pineapple, chicken and bell pepper onto skewers. Place in shallow baking dish.

2. Combine chutney, orange juice, vanilla and nutmeg in small bowl; mix well. Pour over kabobs; cover. Refrigerate up to 4 hours.

3. Preheat broiler. Spray broiler pan with nonstick cooking spray. Place kabobs on prepared broiler pan; discard marinade. Broil kabobs 6 to 8 inches from heat 4 to 5 minutes on each side or until chicken is no longer pink in center. Transfer to serving plates. *Makes 10 servings*

Nutrients per Serving (2 kabobs):
Calories: 108, **Calories from Fat:** 10%, **Total Fat:** 1g,
Saturated Fat: <1g, **Cholesterol:** 21mg, **Sodium:** 22mg,
Carbohydrate: 16g, **Dietary Fiber:** 2g, **Protein:** 8g

Dietary Exchanges: 1 Fruit, 1 Lean Meat

Inside-Out Turkey Sandwiches

2 tablespoons fat-free cream cheese
2 tablespoons pasteurized process cheese spread
2 teaspoons chopped green onion
1 teaspoon prepared mustard
12 thin round slices fat-free turkey breast or smoked turkey breast
4 large pretzel logs or unsalted breadsticks

1. Combine cream cheese, process cheese spread, green onion and mustard in small bowl; mix well.

2. Arrange 3 turkey slices on large sheet of plastic wrap, overlapping slices in center. Spread one fourth of cream cheese mixture evenly onto turkey slices, covering slices completely. Place 1 pretzel at bottom edge of turkey slices; roll up turkey around pretzel. (Be sure to keep all 3 turkey slices together as you roll them around pretzel.)

3. Repeat with remaining ingredients.　　*Makes 4 servings*

Nutrients per Serving (1 sandwich):
Calories: 112, **Calories from Fat:** 18%, **Total Fat:** 2g,
Saturated Fat: 1g, **Cholesterol:** 6mg, **Sodium:** 567mg,
Carbohydrate: 12g, **Dietary Fiber:** <1g, **Protein:** 10g

Dietary Exchanges: 1 Starch, 1 Lean Meat

Grilled Eggplant Roll-Ups

1 tablespoon (½ ounce) hummus
2 slices grilled eggplant
2 tablespoons (½ ounce) crumbled feta cheese
2 tablespoons (½ ounce) chopped green onions
2 slices fresh tomato

Spread hummus on grilled eggplant slices. Top with feta cheese, green onions and tomato. Roll up tightly.   *Makes 1 serving*

Nutrients per Serving (2 roll-ups):
Calories: 99, **Calories from Fat:** 55%, **Total Fat:** 6g, **Saturated Fat:** 3g, **Cholesterol:** 17mg, **Sodium:** 272mg, **Carbohydrate:** 8g, **Dietary Fiber:** 4g, **Protein:** 5g

Dietary Exchanges: 1½ Vegetable, ½ Lean Meat, 1 Fat

Fruit Kabobs with Raspberry Yogurt Dip

½ cup plain fat-free yogurt
¼ cup raspberry fruit spread
1 pint fresh strawberries, hulled
2 cups cubed honeydew melon (1-inch cubes)
2 cups cubed cantaloupe (1-inch cubes)
1 can (8 ounces) pineapple chunks in juice, drained

1. For dip, combine yogurt and fruit spread in small bowl.

2. Thread fruit alternately onto 6 (12-inch) wooden skewers. Serve with dip.   *Makes 6 servings*

Nutrients per Serving (1 kabob with 2 tablespoons dip):
Calories: 108, **Calories from Fat:** 3%, **Total Fat:** <1g, **Saturated Fat:** <1g, **Cholesterol:** <1mg, **Sodium:** 52mg, **Carbohydrate:** 25g, **Dietary Fiber:** 2g, **Protein:** 2g

Dietary Exchanges: 1½ Fruit

Grilled Eggplant Roll-Ups

Grilled Spiced Halibut, Pineapple and Pepper Skewers

2 tablespoons lemon juice or lime juice
1 teaspoon minced garlic
1 teaspoon chili powder
½ teaspoon ground cumin
¼ teaspoon ground cinnamon
⅛ teaspoon ground cloves
½ pound boneless skinless halibut steak, about 1 inch thick
½ small pineapple, peeled, halved lengthwise and cut into 24 pieces
1 large green or red bell pepper, cut into 24 pieces

1. Combine lemon juice, garlic, chili powder, cumin, cinnamon and cloves in large resealable food storage bag; knead until blended.

2. Rinse fish; pat dry. Cut into 12 (1- to 1¼-inch-square) cubes. Add fish to bag. Press out air; seal. Turn gently to coat fish with marinade. Refrigerate 30 minutes to 1 hour. Soak 12 (6- to 8-inch) wooden skewers in water while fish marinates.

3. Alternately thread 2 pieces pineapple, 2 pieces pepper and 1 piece fish onto each skewer.

4. Spray grid with nonstick cooking spray. Place grid 4 to 6 inches above heat. Prepare grill fro direct cooking. Place skewers on grill. Cover or tent with foil; grill over medium-high heat 3 to 4 minutes or until grill marks appear on bottom. Turn skewers over; grill 3 to 4 minutes more or until fish begins to flake when tested with fork.   *Makes 6 servings*

Nutrients per Serving (2 skewers):
Calories: 84, **Calories from Fat:** 13%, **Total Fat:** 1g,
Saturated Fat: <1g, **Cholesterol:** 12mg, **Sodium:** 23mg,
Carbohydrate: 11g, **Dietary Fiber:** 1g, **Protein:** 8g

Dietary Exchanges: ½ Fruit, 1 Lean Meat

Grilled Spiced Halibut, Pineapple
and Pepper Skewers

stuffed
& topped

Mediterranean Roasted Tomatoes

2 small to medium beefsteak tomatoes, cut in half crosswise
4 fresh basil leaves
2 tablespoons finely chopped pitted kalamata olives
2 tablespoons shredded reduced-fat mozzarella cheese
2 tablespoons grated Parmesan cheese

1. Preheat toaster oven to broil. Place tomato halves on rack on toaster oven tray or broiler pan. Top each tomato half with 1 fresh basil leaf, one-fourth olives, one-fourth mozzarella cheese and one-fourth Parmesan cheese.

2. Broil 2 minutes or until cheese melts and begins to brown. Let cool slightly before serving.   *Makes 4 servings*

Nutrients per Serving (1 tomato half):
Calories: 34, **Calories from Fat:** 53%, **Total Fat:** 2g, **Saturated Fat:** 1g, **Cholesterol:** 4mg, **Sodium:** 162mg, **Carbohydrate:** 3g, **Dietary Fiber:** 1g, **Protein:** 2g

Dietary Exchanges: ½ Vegetable, ½ Fat

Easy Nachos

4 (6-inch) flour tortillas
   Nonstick cooking spray
4 ounces lean ground turkey
⅔ cup salsa (mild or medium)
2 tablespoons sliced green onion
**½ cup (2 ounces) shredded reduced-fat Cheddar
   cheese**

1. Preheat oven to 350°F. Cut each tortilla into 8 wedges; lightly spray one side of wedges with cooking spray. Place on ungreased baking sheet. Bake 5 to 9 minutes or until lightly browned and crisp.

2. Meanwhile, brown turkey in small nonstick skillet over medium-high heat, stirring to break up meat. Drain fat. Stir in salsa; cook until hot.

3. Spoon turkey mixture over tortilla wedges. Sprinkle with green onion. Top with cheese. Return to oven 1 to 2 minutes or until cheese melts. *Makes 4 servings*

Serving Suggestion: To make these nachos even more special, cut tortillas into shapes with cookie cutters and bake as directed.

Tip: In a hurry? Substitute baked corn chips for flour tortillas and cooking spray. Proceed as directed.

Nutrients per Serving (8 nachos):
Calories: 209, **Calories from Fat:** 32%, **Total Fat:** 7g, **Saturated Fat:** 2g, **Cholesterol:** 29mg, **Sodium:** 703mg, **Carbohydrate:** 23g, **Dietary Fiber:** 2g, **Protein:** 12g

Dietary Exchanges: 1 Starch, 1 Vegetable, 1 Lean Meat, 1 Fat

Easy Nachos

Bruschetta

Nonstick cooking spray
1 cup thinly sliced onion
½ cup chopped seeded tomato
2 tablespoons capers, drained
¼ teaspoon black pepper
3 cloves garlic, finely chopped
1 teaspoon olive oil
4 slices French bread
½ cup (2 ounces) shredded reduced-fat Monterey
   Jack cheese

1. Spray large nonstick skillet with cooking spray. Cook and stir onion over medium heat 5 minutes. Stir in tomato, capers and pepper. Cook 3 minutes.

2. Preheat broiler. Combine garlic and olive oil in small bowl. Brush bread slices with oil mixture. Top with onion mixture; sprinkle with cheese. Place on baking sheet. Broil 3 minutes or until cheese melts. *Makes 4 servings*

Nutrients per Serving (1 bruschetta slice):
Calories: 90, **Calories from Fat:** 20%, **Total Fat:** 2g,
Saturated Fat: <1g, **Cholesterol:** 0mg, **Sodium:** 194mg,
Carbohydrate: 17g, **Dietary Fiber:** <1g, **Protein:** 3g

Dietary Exchanges: 1 Starch, ½ Lean Meat

Tortilla "Pizza"

1 can (about 14 ounces) Mexican-style stewed
   tomatoes, drained
1 can (10 ounces) chunk white chicken packed in
   water, drained
1 green onion, minced
2 teaspoons ground cumin, divided
½ teaspoon garlic powder
1 cup fat-free refried beans
¼ cup chopped fresh cilantro, divided
2 large or 4 small flour tortillas
1 cup (4 ounces) shredded Monterey Jack cheese with
   jalapeño peppers

1. Preheat broiler. Combine tomatoes, chicken, green onion,
1 teaspoon cumin and garlic powder in medium bowl; mix well.

2. Combine refried beans, remaining 1 teaspoon cumin and
2 tablespoons cilantro in small bowl. Set aside.

3. Place tortillas on baking sheet. Broil 30 seconds to 1 minute
per side or until crisp but not browned. Remove from oven.
Reduce oven temperature to 400°F. Spread bean mixture
evenly over each tortilla. Top with chicken mixture and cheese.
Bake 5 minutes.

4. *Turn oven to broil.* Broil tortillas 2 to 3 minutes or until
cheese melts. Top with remaining cilantro. Serve immediately.

Makes 8 servings

Nutrients per Serving (1 wedge [¼ of 1 large Tortilla "Pizza" or ½ of
1 small Tortilla "Pizza"]):
Calories: 170, **Calories from Fat:** 42%, **Total Fat:** 8g,
Saturated Fat: 4g, **Cholesterol:** 35mg, **Sodium:** 457mg,
Carbohydrate: 11g, **Dietary Fiber:** 2g, **Protein:** 13g

Dietary Exchanges: ½ Starch, ½ Vegetable, 1½ Lean Meat, 1 Fat

Tortilla "Pizza"

Blue Crab Stuffed Tomatoes

½ pound Florida blue crabmeat
10 plum tomatoes
½ cup finely chopped celery
⅓ cup plain low-fat yogurt
2 tablespoons minced green onion
2 tablespoons finely chopped red bell pepper
½ teaspoon lemon juice
¼ teaspoon salt
⅛ teaspoon black pepper

Remove any shell or cartilage from crabmeat.

Cut tomatoes in half lengthwise. Carefully scoop out centers of tomatoes; discard pulp. Invert on paper towels.

Combine crabmeat, celery, yogurt, onion, red pepper, lemon juice, salt and black pepper. Mix well.

Fill tomato halves with crab mixture. Refrigerate 2 hours.

Makes 20 appetizers

Favorite recipe from **Florida Department of Agriculture and Consumer Services, Bureau of Seafood and Aquaculture**

Nutrients per Serving (1 stuffed tomato):
Calories: 46, **Calories from Fat:** 12%, **Total Fat:** 1g,
Saturated Fat: <1g, **Cholesterol:** 27mg, **Sodium:** 138mg,
Carbohydrate: 3g, **Dietary Fiber:** 1g, **Protein:** 7g

Dietary Exchanges: ½ Vegetable, 1 Lean Meat

Cheesy Potato Skin Appetizers

⅔ **cup Zesty Pico de Gallo (page 68) or purchased**
   salsa
 5 **potatoes (4 to 5 ounces each)**
   Butter-flavored cooking spray
½ **(8-ounce) package cream cheese**
 2 **tablespoons reduced-fat sour cream**
⅓ **cup shredded reduced-fat sharp Cheddar cheese**
 2 **tablespoons sliced black olives (optional)**
¼ **cup minced fresh cilantro**

1. Prepare Zesty Pico de Gallo; set aside.

2. Preheat oven to 425°F. Scrub potatoes; pierce several times with fork. Bake 45 minutes or until soft. Cool.

3. Cut each potato in half lengthwise. Scoop out potato with spoon, leaving ¼-inch-thick shell. (Reserve potato for another use, if desired.) Place potato skins on baking sheet; spray lightly with cooking spray.

4. Preheat broiler. Broil potato skins 6 inches from heat, 5 minutes or until lightly browned and crisp.

5. Preheat oven to 350°F. Combine cream cheese and sour cream in small bowl; stir until well blended. Divide evenly among potato skins; spread to cover. Top with Zesty Pico de Gallo, cheese and olives, if desired. Bake 15 minutes or until heated through. Sprinkle with cilantro.   *Makes 10 servings*

continued on page 68

stuffed & topped

Cheesy Potato Skin Appetizers, continued

Zesty Pico de Gallo

   2 cups chopped seeded tomatoes
   1 cup chopped green onions
   1 can (8 ounces) tomato sauce
   ½ cup minced fresh cilantro
   1 to 2 tablespoons minced jalapeño peppers*
   1 tablespoon fresh lime juice

*Jalapeño peppers can sting and irritate the skin, so wear rubber gloves when handling peppers and do not touch your eyes.

Combine all ingredients in medium bowl. Cover and refrigerate at least 1 hour. *Makes 4 cups*

Nutrients per Serving (1 appetizer with about 1 tablespoon pico de gallo):
Calories: 86, **Calories from Fat:** 10%, **Total Fat:** 1g,
Saturated Fat: 1g, **Cholesterol:** 4mg, **Sodium:** 149mg,
Carbohydrate: 15g, **Dietary Fiber:** 3g, **Protein:** 4g

Dietary Exchanges: 1 Starch

Instant Individual Pizza

   1 (6-inch) whole wheat tortilla
   1 tablespoon no-salt-added tomato sauce
   ¼ teaspoon dried oregano
   2 tablespoons shredded reduced-fat Swiss cheese

Preheat oven to 500°F. Place tortilla on baking sheet. Spread tortilla to edges with tomato sauce. Sprinkle with oregano. Top with cheese. Bake 5 minutes or until tortilla is crisp and cheese is bubbly. *Makes 1 serving*

Nutrients per Serving (1 pizza):
Calories: 106, **Calories from Fat:** 19%, **Total Fat:** 2g,
Saturated Fat: 1g, **Cholesterol:** 8mg, **Sodium:** 208mg,
Carbohydrate: 13g, **Dietary Fiber:** 9g, **Protein:** 7g

Dietary Exchanges: 1 Starch, ½ Lean Meat

Super Nachos

12 large baked low-fat tortilla chips (about 1½ ounces)
½ cup (2 ounces) shredded reduced-fat Cheddar
    cheese
¼ cup fat-free refried beans
2 tablespoons chunky salsa

MICROWAVE DIRECTIONS

1. Arrange chips in single layer on large microwavable plate. Sprinkle cheese evenly over chips.

2. Spoon 1 teaspoon beans over each chip; top with ½ teaspoon salsa.

3. Microwave on MEDIUM (50%) 1½ minutes; rotate dish.* Microwave 1 to 1½ minutes more or until cheese is melted.

Makes 2 servings

This recipe was tested in a 1100-watt microwave oven.

Conventional Directions: Preheat oven to 350°F. Substitute foil-covered baking sheet for microwavable plate. Assemble nachos on prepared baking sheet as directed above. Bake 10 to 12 minutes or until cheese is melted.

Tip: For a single serving of nachos, arrange 6 large tortilla chips on microwavable plate; top each chip with 2 teaspoons cheese, 1 teaspoon refried beans and ½ teaspoon salsa. Microwave on MEDIUM (50%) 1 minute; rotate dish. Microwave 30 seconds to 1 minute or until cheese is melted.

Nutrients per Serving (6 nachos):
Calories: 176, **Calories from Fat:** 26%, **Total Fat:** 5g, **Saturated Fat:** 2g, **Cholesterol:** 16mg, **Sodium:** 683mg, **Carbohydrate:** 23g, **Dietary Fiber:** 2g, **Protein:** 10g

Dietary Exchanges: 1½ Starch, 1 Lean Meat

BLT Cukes

3 slices crisp-cooked bacon, chopped
½ cup finely chopped lettuce
½ cup finely chopped baby spinach
¼ cup diced tomato
1 tablespoon plus 1½ teaspoons fat-free mayonnaise
Pinch salt
¼ teaspoon black pepper
1 large cucumber
Minced fresh parsley or green onion (optional)

1. Combine bacon, lettuce, spinach, tomato and mayonnaise. Season with salt and pepper; set aside.

2. Peel cucumber. Trim off ends and cut in half lengthwise. Use spoon to scoop out seeds; discard seeds. Divide bacon mixture between cucumber halves, mounding in hollowed areas. Garnish with parsley. Cut into 2-inch pieces.

Makes 8 to 10 pieces

Note: Make these snacks when cucumbers are plentiful and large enough to easily hollow out with a spoon. You can make these up to 12 hours ahead of time.

Nutrients per Serving (1 piece):
Calories: 26, **Calories from Fat:** 50%, **Total Fat:** 2g,
Saturated Fat: <1g, **Cholesterol:** 3mg, **Sodium:** 72mg,
Carbohydrate: 2g, **Dietary Fiber:** <1g, **Protein:** 2g

Dietary Exchanges: Free

BLT Cukes

Crabmeat Crostini

**1 pound Florida blue crabmeat or stone crabmeat
1½ cups shredded low-fat mozzarella cheese
½ cup Florida pecan pieces, toasted and chopped
2 Florida datil peppers, seeded and chopped (or other hot peppers)
2 teaspoons chopped fresh Florida rosemary leaves
2 teaspoons chopped fresh Florida thyme leaves
1 (3-ounce) package sun-dried tomatoes, rehydrated and chopped
12 (1-inch-thick) slices French bread, sliced diagonally**

Remove any shell or cartilage from crabmeat. Combine all ingredients except bread; mix well. Cover and refrigerate for 1 hour. Arrange bread slices on baking sheet and place equal portions of crab mixture on each slice. Broil 4 to 6 inches from source of heat for 6 to 8 minutes or until cheese melts or begins to brown. *Makes 12 appetizer servings*

Favorite recipe from **Florida Department of Agriculture and Consumer Services, Bureau of Seafood and Aquaculture**

Nutrients per Serving (1 crostini):
Calories: 202, **Calories from Fat:** 33%, **Total Fat:** 7g, **Saturated Fat:** 2g, **Cholesterol:** 40mg, **Sodium:** 516mg, **Carbohydrate:** 20g, **Dietary Fiber:** 2g, **Protein:** 15g

Dietary Exchanges: 1 Starch, 1 Vegetable, 1½ Lean Meat, ½ Fat

Quick Pimiento Cheese Snacks

2 ounces reduced-fat cream cheese, softened
½ cup (2 ounces) shredded reduced-fat Cheddar cheese
1 jar (2 ounces) diced pimientos, drained
2 tablespoons finely chopped pecans
½ teaspoon hot pepper sauce
24 (¼-inch-thick) French bread slices or party bread slices

1. Preheat broiler.

2. Combine cream cheese and Cheddar cheese in small bowl; mix well. Stir in pimientos, pecans and pepper sauce.

3. Place bread slices on broiler pan or nonstick baking sheet. Broil 4 inches from heat 1 to 2 minutes or until lightly toasted on both sides.

4. Spread cheese mixture evenly onto bread slices. Broil 1 to 2 minutes or until cheese mixture is hot and bubbly. Transfer to serving plate. *Makes 24 servings*

Nutrients per Serving (1 snack):
Calories: 86, **Calories from Fat:** 22%, **Total Fat:** 2g, **Saturated Fat:** 1g, **Cholesterol:** 3mg, **Sodium:** 195mg, **Carbohydrate:** 14g, **Dietary Fiber:** <1g, **Protein:** 3g

Dietary Exchanges: 1 Starch, ½ Fat

Quick Pimiento Cheese Snacks

Stuffed Party Baguette

2 medium red bell peppers
1 loaf French bread (about 14 inches long)
¼ cup plus 2 tablespoons fat-free Italian dressing, divided
1 small red onion, very thinly sliced
8 large fresh basil leaves
3 ounces Swiss cheese, very thinly sliced

1. Preheat oven to 425°F. Cover large baking sheet with foil; set aside.

2. To roast bell peppers, cut in half; remove stems, seeds and membranes. Place peppers, cut sides down, on prepared baking sheet. Bake 20 to 25 minutes or until skins are browned.

3. Transfer peppers to paper bag; close bag. Let stand 10 minutes or until peppers are cool enough to handle and skins are loosened. Peel off and discard skins; cut peppers into strips.

4. Trim ends from bread. Cut loaf in half lengthwise. Remove soft insides of loaf and reserve for another use.

5. Brush ¼ cup Italian dressing evenly onto cut sides of bread. Arrange pepper strips on bottom half of loaf; top with onion. Brush onion with remaining 2 tablespoons Italian dressing; top with basil and cheese. Replace bread top. Wrap loaf tightly in plastic wrap; refrigerate at least 2 hours.

6. To serve, remove plastic wrap. Cut loaf crosswise into 1-inch slices. Secure with toothpicks. *Makes 12 servings*

Nutrients per Serving (1 baguette slice):
Calories: 98, **Calories from Fat:** 25%, **Total Fat:** 3g,
Saturated Fat: 1g, **Cholesterol:** 7mg, **Sodium:** 239mg,
Carbohydrate: 14g, **Dietary Fiber:** 1g, **Protein:** 4g

Dietary Exchanges: 1 Starch, ½ Fat

Stuffed Party Baguette

Tomato and Caper Crostini

1 French roll, cut into 8 slices
2 plum tomatoes, finely chopped (about 4 ounces)
1 tablespoon plus 1½ teaspoons capers, drained
1½ teaspoons dried basil
1 teaspoon extra-virgin olive oil
1 ounce crumbled feta cheese with sun-dried
tomatoes and basil, or any variety

1. Preheat oven to 350°F.

2. Place bread slices on ungreased baking sheet in single layer. Bake 15 minutes or just until golden brown. Cool completely.

3. Meanwhile, combine tomatoes, capers, basil and oil in small bowl; mix well.

4. Just before serving, spoon tomato mixture on each bread slice; sprinkle with cheese. *Makes 2 servings*

Nutrients per Serving (4 crostini with ½ cup tomato mixture [1 tablespoon per crostini]):
Calories: 123, **Calories from Fat:** 44%, **Total Fat:** 6g, **Saturated Fat:** 3g, **Cholesterol:** 12mg, **Sodium:** 466mg, **Carbohydrate:** 13g, **Dietary Fiber:** 2g, **Protein:** 4g

Dietary Exchanges: 1 Starch, 1 Fat

tip

Capers are the small, pea-sized bud of a flower from the caper bush. Capers add color and flavor to any Mediterranean dish. If you are watching your sodium intake, be sure to rinse the capers before adding them.

Mediterranean Pita Pizzas

2 (8-inch) rounds pita bread
1 teaspoon olive oil
1 cup canned cannellini beans, rinsed and drained
2 teaspoons lemon juice
2 cloves garlic, minced
½ cup thinly sliced radicchio or escarole lettuce
    (optional)
½ cup chopped seeded tomato
½ cup finely chopped red onion
¼ cup (1 ounce) crumbled feta cheese
2 tablespoons sliced pitted black olives

1. Preheat oven to 450°F. Arrange pitas on baking sheet; brush tops with oil. Bake 6 minutes.

2. Meanwhile, place beans in small bowl; mash lightly with fork. Stir in lemon juice and garlic.

3. Spread bean mixture evenly onto pita rounds to within ½ inch of edges. Arrange remaining ingredients on pitas. Bake 5 minutes or until topping is thoroughly heated and crust is crisp. Cut into wedges; serve hot.   *Makes 8 servings*

Nutrients per Serving (1 pizza wedge):
Calories: 98, **Calories from Fat:** 29%, **Total Fat:** 3g,
Saturated Fat: 1g, **Cholesterol:** 7mg, **Sodium:** 282mg,
Carbohydrate: 14g, **Dietary Fiber:** 2g, **Protein:** 4g

Dietary Exchanges: 1 Starch, ½ Fat

Marinated Artichoke Cheese Toasts

1 jar (8 ounces) marinated artichoke hearts, drained
½ cup (2 ounces) shredded reduced-fat Swiss cheese
⅓ cup finely chopped roasted red peppers
⅓ cup finely chopped celery
1 tablespoon plus 1½ teaspoons reduced-fat mayonnaise
24 melba toast rounds
Paprika

1. Rinse artichokes under cold running water; drain well. Pat dry with paper towels. Finely chop artichokes; place in medium bowl. Add cheese, peppers, celery and mayonnaise; mix well.

2. Spoon artichoke mixture evenly onto melba toast rounds; place on large nonstick baking sheet or broiler pan. Broil 6 inches from heat 45 seconds or until cheese mixture is hot and bubbly. Garnish with paprika. *Makes 12 servings*

Nutrients per Serving (2 toasts):
Calories: 57, **Calories from Fat:** 23%, **Total Fat:** 1g,
Saturated Fat: 1g, **Cholesterol:** 4mg, **Sodium:** 65mg,
Carbohydrate: 7g, **Dietary Fiber:** 1g, **Protein:** 4g

Dietary Exchanges: ½ Starch

tip

Melba toast is made by slicing day-old bread into very thin slices, trimming the crust and baking the slices in an oven at a low temperature until they are pale golden brown and crisp. They are a great base for appetizers!

Smoked Chicken Bagel Snacks

⅓ cup fat-free cream cheese, softened
2 teaspoons spicy brown mustard
¼ cup chopped roasted red peppers
1 green onion, sliced
5 mini bagels, split
3 ounces smoked chicken or turkey, cut into 10 very thin slices
¼ medium cucumber, cut into 10 thin slices

1. Combine cream cheese and mustard in small bowl; mix well. Stir in peppers and green onion.

2. Spread cream cheese mixture evenly onto cut sides of bagels. Cover bottom halves of bagels with chicken, folding chicken to fit onto bagels. Top with cucumber slices and bagel tops.   *Makes 5 servings*

Nutrients per Serving (1 Bagel Snack):
Calories: 139, **Calories from Fat:** 7%, **Total Fat:** 1g, **Saturated Fat:** <1g, **Cholesterol:** 12mg, **Sodium:** 502mg, **Carbohydrate:** 21g, **Dietary Fiber:** <1g, **Protein:** 10g

Dietary Exchanges: 1½ Starch, 1 Lean Meat

by the handful

Rosemary-Scented Nut Mix

2 tablespoons unsalted butter
2 cups pecan halves
1 cup unsalted macadamia nuts
1 cup walnuts
1 teaspoon dried rosemary, crushed
½ teaspoon salt
¼ teaspoon red pepper flakes

1. Preheat oven to 300°F. Melt butter in large saucepan over low heat. Add pecans, macadamia nuts and walnuts; mix well. Add rosemary, salt and red pepper flakes; cook and stir about 1 minute.

2. Spread mixture onto ungreased nonstick baking sheet. Bake 15 minutes, stirring mixture occasionally. Cool completely in pan on wire rack.   *Makes 32 servings*

Nutrients per Serving (2 tablespoons mix):
Calories: 108, **Calories from Fat:** 88%, **Total Fat:** 11g, **Saturated Fat:** 2g, **Cholesterol:** 2mg, **Sodium:** 37mg, **Carbohydrate:** 2g, **Dietary Fiber:** 1g, **Protein:** 2g

Dietary Exchanges: 2 Fat

Peppy Snack Mix

 3 (3-inch) plain rice cakes, broken into bite-size
    pieces
1½ cups bite-size frosted shredded wheat biscuit cereal
 ¾ cup pretzel sticks, halved
 3 tablespoons reduced-fat margarine, melted
 2 teaspoons reduced-sodium Worcestershire sauce
 ¾ teaspoon chili powder
 ⅛ to ¼ teaspoon ground red pepper

Preheat oven to 300°F. Combine rice cake pieces, cereal and pretzels in 13×9-inch baking pan. Combine margarine, Worcestershire, chili powder and pepper in small bowl. Drizzle over cereal mixture; toss to combine. Bake 20 minutes, stirring after 10 minutes. *Makes 6 (⅔-cup) servings*

Nutrients per Serving (⅔ cup snack mix):
Calories: 118, **Calories from Fat:** 25%, **Total Fat:** 3g,
Saturated Fat: 1g, **Cholesterol:** 0mg, **Sodium:** 156mg,
Carbohydrate: 20g, **Dietary Fiber:** 1g, **Protein:** 2g

Dietary Exchanges: 1½ Starch, ½ Fat

tip

Worcestershire sauce is a dark, savory sauce developed in India and named after the English town, Worcester, where it was first bottled. It has a very unique, complex flavor that is difficult to substitute.

Cinnamon Caramel Corn

8 cups air-popped popcorn (about ⅓ cup kernels)
2 tablespoons honey
4 teaspoons butter
¼ teaspoon ground cinnamon

1. Preheat oven to 350°F. Spray jelly-roll pan with nonstick cooking spray. Place popcorn in large bowl.

2. Stir honey, butter and cinnamon in small saucepan over low heat until butter is melted and mixture is smooth; immediately pour over popcorn. Toss with spoon to coat evenly. Pour onto prepared pan; bake 12 to 14 minutes or until coating is golden brown and appears crackled, stirring twice.

3. Let cool on pan 5 minutes. (As popcorn cools, coating becomes crisp. If not crisp enough, or if popcorn softens upon standing, return to oven and heat 5 to 8 minutes.)

Makes 4 servings

Cajun Popcorn: Preheat oven and prepare jelly-roll pan as directed above. Combine 7 teaspoons honey, 4 teaspoons butter and 1 teaspoon Cajun or Creole seasoning in small saucepan. Proceed with recipe as directed above. Makes 4 servings.

Italian Popcorn: Spray 8 cups of air-popped popcorn with fat-free butter-flavored spray to coat. Sprinkle with 2 tablespoons finely grated Parmesan cheese, ⅛ teaspoon black pepper and ½ teaspoon dried oregano leaves. Gently toss to coat. Makes 4 servings.

Nutrients per Serving (2 cups Cinnamon Caramel Corn):
Calories: 117, **Calories from Fat:** 29%, **Total Fat:** 4g, **Saturated Fat:** 1g, **Cholesterol:** 0mg, **Sodium:** 45mg, **Carbohydrate:** 19g, **Dietary Fiber:** 1g, **Protein:** 2g

Dietary Exchanges: 1 Starch, 1 Fat

Clockwise from top: Italian Popcorn, Cinnamon Caramel Corn and Cajun Popcorn

Bite-You-Back Roasted Edamame

2 teaspoons vegetable oil
2 teaspoons honey
¼ teaspoon wasabi powder*
1 package (10 ounces) ready-to-eat shelled edamame

Available in the Asian section of most supermarkets and in Asian specialty markets.

1. Preheat oven to 375°F.

2. Stir together oil, honey and wasabi powder in large bowl. Add edamame and toss to coat. Transfer to baking sheet and arrange in single layer.

3. Bake for 12 to 15 minutes or until edamame are golden brown, stirring once. Remove from baking sheet immediately; sprinkle with salt, if desired.

4. Cool completely and store in airtight container until ready to serve.   *Makes 4 servings*

Nutrients per Serving (½ cup [without added salt]):
Calories: 78, **Calories from Fat:** 29%, **Total Fat:** 4g, **Saturated Fat:** 1g, **Cholesterol:** 0mg, **Sodium:** 7mg, **Carbohydrate:** 7g, **Dietary Fiber:** 1g, **Protein:** 4g

Dietary Exchanges: 1½ Vegetable, ½ Fat

Southwest Snack Mix

    4 cups corn cereal squares
    2 cups unsalted pretzels
    ½ cup unsalted pumpkin or squash seeds
 1½ teaspoons chili powder
    1 teaspoon minced fresh cilantro or parsley
    ½ teaspoon garlic powder
    ½ teaspoon onion powder
    1 egg white
    2 tablespoons olive oil
    2 tablespoons lime juice

1. Preheat oven to 300°F. Spray large nonstick baking sheet with nonstick cooking spray.

2. Combine cereal, pretzels and pumpkin seeds in large bowl. Combine chili powder, cilantro, garlic powder and onion powder in small bowl.

3. Whisk together egg white, oil and lime juice in separate small bowl. Pour over cereal mixture; toss to coat evenly. Add seasoning mixture; mix lightly to coat evenly. Transfer to prepared baking sheet.

4. Bake 45 minutes, stirring every 15 minutes; cool. Store in airtight container.   *Makes about 12 servings*

Variation: Substitute ½ cup unsalted peanuts for pumpkin seeds.

Nutrients per Serving (½ cup snack mix):
Calories: 93, **Calories from Fat:** 28%, **Total Fat:** 3g,
Saturated Fat: <1g, **Cholesterol:** 0mg, **Sodium:** 114mg,
Carbohydrate: 15g, **Dietary Fiber:** 1g, **Protein:** 2g

Dietary Exchanges: 1 Starch, ½ Fat

Taco Popcorn Olé

9 cups air-popped popcorn
   Butter-flavored cooking spray
1 teaspoon chili powder
½ teaspoon salt
½ teaspoon garlic powder
⅛ teaspoon ground red pepper (optional)

1. Preheat oven to 350°F. Line 15×10-inch jelly-roll pan with foil.

2. Place popcorn in single layer on prepared pan. Coat lightly with cooking spray.

3. Combine chili powder, salt, garlic powder and red pepper, if desired, in small bowl; sprinkle over popcorn. Mix lightly to coat evenly.

4. Bake 5 minutes or until hot, stirring gently after 3 minutes. Spread mixture in single layer on large sheet of foil to cool.

Makes 6 servings

Tip: Store popcorn mixture in tightly covered container at room temperature up to 4 days.

Nutrients per Serving (1½ cups):
Calories: 48, **Calories from Fat:** 10%, **Total Fat:** 1g,
Saturated Fat: <1g, **Cholesterol:** 0mg, **Sodium:** 199mg,
Carbohydrate: 10g, **Dietary Fiber:** 2g, **Protein:** 2g

Dietary Exchanges: ½ Starch

Taco Popcorn Olé

Sweet & Spicy Whole-Grain Snack Mix

1 egg white
¼ cup sugar substitute*
1 tablespoon soy sauce
¼ teaspoon ground red pepper
2 cups spoon-size shredded wheat cereal
2 cups wheat cereal squares
2 cups unsalted mini-pretzel twists
¼ cup dry-roasted unsalted peanuts

This recipe was tested with sucralose-based sugar substitute.

1. Preheat oven to 300° F. Spray large nonstick baking pan with nonstick cooking spray; set aside.

2. Place egg white in large bowl; whisk until foamy. Whisk in sugar substitute, soy sauce and red pepper.

3. Combine cereals, pretzels and peanuts in medium bowl. Add to egg white mixture; toss to coat. Spread in even layer on prepared pan; bake 30 minutes, stirring every 10 minutes, until crispy. Cool completely on pan on wire rack. Store in airtight container for up to 1 week.   *Makes 10 servings*

Nutrients per Serving (½ cup snack mix):
Calories: 127, **Calories from Fat:** 17%, **Total Fat:** 3g,
Saturated Fat: <1g, **Cholesterol:** 0mg, **Sodium:** 216mg,
Carbohydrate: 24g, **Dietary Fiber:** 3g, **Protein:** 4g

Dietary Exchanges: 1½ Starch, ½ Fat

main dishes
contents

beef
& pork

Tex-Mex Flank Steak Salad

½ beef flank steak (about 6 ounces)
½ teaspoon Mexican seasoning blend or chili powder
⅛ teaspoon salt
   Olive oil cooking spray
4 cups packaged mixed salad greens
1 can (11 ounces) mandarin orange sections, drained
2 tablespoons green taco sauce

1. Cut flank steak lengthwise in half, then crosswise into thin strips. Combine steak, Mexican seasoning and salt in medium bowl; toss to coat.

2. Lightly spray large skillet with cooking spray. Heat over medium-high heat. Add steak; cook and stir 1 to 2 minutes or until desired doneness.

3. Toss together greens and orange sections. Arrange on serving plates. Top with warm steak; drizzle with taco sauce.

Makes 2 servings

Nutrients per Serving (½ of total recipe):
Calories: 240, **Calories from Fat:** 25%, **Total Fat:** 7g,
Saturated Fat: 3g, **Cholesterol:** 37mg, **Sodium:** 388mg,
Carbohydrate: 21g, **Dietary Fiber:** 2g, **Protein:** 25g

Dietary Exchanges: ½ Fruit, 2½ Vegetable, 2½ Lean Meat

Pork and Plum Kabobs

¾ **pound boneless pork loin chops (1 inch thick),
    trimmed of fat and cut into 1-inch pieces**
1½ **teaspoons ground cumin**
 ½ **teaspoon ground cinnamon**
 ¼ **teaspoon salt**
 ¼ **teaspoon garlic powder**
 ¼ **teaspoon ground red pepper**
 ¼ **cup sliced green onions**
 ¼ **cup red raspberry fruit spread**
 1 **tablespoon orange juice**
 3 **plums, pitted and cut into wedges**

1. Place pork in large resealable food storage bag. Combine cumin, cinnamon, salt, garlic powder and red pepper in small bowl; sprinkle over meat in bag. Shake to coat meat with spices.

2. Prepare grill for direct grilling. Combine green onions, raspberry spread and orange juice in small bowl; set aside.

3. Alternately thread pork and plum wedges onto 8 skewers.* Grill kabobs directly over medium heat 12 to 14 minutes or until meat is barely pink in center, turning once during grilling. Brush frequently with raspberry mixture during last 5 minutes of grilling. *Makes 4 servings*

If using wooden skewers, soak in water 20 minutes before using to prevent burning.

Prep Time: 10 minutes
Grill Time: 12 to 14 minutes

Nutrients per Serving (2 kabobs):
Calories: 191, **Calories from Fat:** 23%, **Total Fat:** 5g,
Saturated Fat: 2g, **Cholesterol:** 53mg, **Sodium:** 183mg,
Carbohydrate: 17g, **Dietary Fiber:** 1g, **Protein:** 19g

Dietary Exchanges: 1 Fruit, 2½ Lean Meat

Favorite Beef Stew

   3 medium carrots, cut lengthwise in half, then cut into
       1-inch pieces
   3 stalks celery, cut into 1-inch pieces
   2 large potatoes, peeled and cut into ½-inch pieces
1½ cups chopped onions
   3 cloves garlic, chopped
4½ teaspoons Worcestershire sauce
   ¾ teaspoon *each* dried thyme and dried basil
   ½ teaspoon black pepper
   1 bay leaf
   2 pounds beef stew meat (1-inch pieces)
   1 can (about 14 ounces) diced tomatoes
   1 can (about 14 ounces) fat-free reduced-sodium
       beef broth
   ½ cup cold water
   ¼ cup all-purpose flour

SLOW COOKER DIRECTIONS

1. Layer ingredients in slow cooker in the following order: carrots, celery, potatoes, onions, garlic, Worcestershire sauce, thyme, basil, pepper, bay leaf, beef, tomatoes and broth.

2. Cover and cook on LOW 8 to 9 hours.

3. Remove beef and vegetables to large serving bowl; cover and keep warm. Remove and discard bay leaf. Increase heat to HIGH. Blend water and flour in small bowl until smooth. Add ½ cup cooking liquid; mix well. Stir flour mixture into slow cooker. Cover and cook 15 minutes or until thickened. Pour sauce over meat and vegetables. Serve immediately.

Makes 8 servings

Nutrients per Serving (1 bowl of stew [⅛ of total recipe]):
Calories: 276, **Calories from Fat:** 20%, **Total Fat:** 8g,
Saturated Fat: 3g, **Cholesterol:** 70mg, **Sodium:** 266mg,
Carbohydrate: 25g, **Dietary Fiber:** 3g, **Protein:** 25g

Dietary Exchanges: 1 Starch, 1½ Vegetable, 3 Lean Meat

Butternut Gratin

1 butternut squash
6 ounces lean boneless pork chops, trimmed of fat,
 cooked and cut into bite-size pieces (4 ounces
 cooked weight)
½ cup chopped celery
½ cup vegetable broth
⅓ cup whole grain bread crumbs
¼ cup sliced green onions
 2 tablespoons shredded reduced-fat Cheddar cheese
¼ teaspoon black pepper (optional)

MICROWAVE DIRECTIONS

1. Pierce squash with knife tip in several places. Microwave on HIGH 15 to 20 minutes or until squash is barely tender.

2. Remove squash from microwave and let rest about 5 minutes or until cool enough to handle. Cut off top and discard. Slice squash in half lengthwise and scoop out seeds. Use knife to score each half into a grid of 1-inch cubes, leaving skin intact. Then slice cubes from skin.

3. Lightly coat microwavable baking dish with nonstick cooking spray. Combine squash, pork, celery, broth, crumbs and green onions in prepared dish. Top with cheese. Microwave on HIGH for 2 to 2½ minutes or until squash is tender and heated through. Season with pepper, if desired.   *Makes 2 servings*

Nutrients per Serving (1¾ cups Butternut Gratin):
Calories: 285, **Calories from Fat:** 25%, **Total Fat:** 8g,
Saturated Fat: 3g, **Cholesterol:** 83mg, **Sodium:** 452mg,
Carbohydrate: 23g, **Dietary Fiber:** 5g, **Protein:** 31g

Dietary Exchanges: 1½ Starch, ½ Vegetable, 3½ Lean Meat

Stuffed Eggplant

        Nonstick cooking spray
     2 eggplants (about 8 ounces each), halved lengthwise
     ½ teaspoon salt
   1½ teaspoons chopped garlic
     1 teaspoon black pepper
     1 pound boneless beef sirloin steak, trimmed of
           visible fat and cut into ¼-inch strips
     2 cups sliced red and green bell peppers
     2 cups sliced mushrooms
     ¼ cup water
        Pinch paprika and chopped fresh parsley (optional)

1. Preheat oven to 450°F. Spray baking dish with cooking spray.

2. Place eggplant halves cut side up in large baking dish; pierce with a fork in approximately 8 places. Sprinkle each eggplant half with ⅛ teaspoon salt. Cover with foil; bake 45 minutes.

3. Meanwhile, spray large nonstick skillet with cooking spray. Add garlic and black pepper; cook and stir over medium heat 2 minutes. Add sirloin strips; cook and stir 5 minutes.

4. Add bell peppers; cook 5 minutes. Add mushrooms; cook 5 minutes. Stir in water; cover. Remove skillet from heat.

5. Remove eggplant from oven; let cool 5 minutes. Mash cooked eggplant centers with fork without breaking shells. Top each half with beef mixture; combine with mashed eggplant. Cover with foil; bake 15 minutes. Garnish with paprika and parsley.   *Makes 4 servings*

Nutrients per Serving (1 stuffed eggplant half):
Calories: 195, **Calories from Fat:** 23%, **Total Fat:** 5g,
Saturated Fat: 2g, **Sodium:** 348mg, **Carbohydrate:** 12g,
Dietary Fiber: 4g, **Protein:** 25g

Dietary Exchanges: 2½ Vegetable, 2½ Lean Meat

Browned Pork Chops with Gravy

½ teaspoon dried sage
½ teaspoon dried marjoram
¼ teaspoon black pepper
⅛ teaspoon salt
4 boneless pork loin chops (¾ pound), trimmed of fat
   Olive oil cooking spray
¼ cup chopped onion
1 clove garlic, minced
1 cup sliced mushrooms
¾ cup beef broth
⅓ cup fat-free sour cream
1 tablespoon all-purpose flour
1 teaspoon Dijon mustard
2 cups hot cooked yolk-free wide egg noodles
   Chopped fresh parsley (optional)

1. Combine sage, marjoram, pepper and salt in small bowl. Rub onto both sides of pork chops. Spray large nonstick skillet with cooking spray; heat over medium heat. Place chops in skillet. Cook 5 minutes, turning once, or until chops are just barely pink. Remove chops from skillet; keep warm.

2. Add onion and garlic to skillet; cook and stir 2 minutes. Add mushrooms and broth. Bring to a boil. Reduce heat; simmer, covered, 3 to 4 minutes or until mushrooms are tender.

3. Whisk together sour cream, flour and mustard in medium bowl. Whisk in about 3 tablespoons broth mixture from skillet. Stir sour cream mixture into skillet. Cook, stirring constantly, until mixture comes to a boil. Serve gravy over pork chops and noodles. Garnish with parsley.   *Makes 4 servings*

Nutrients per Serving (1 pork chop with ½ cup noodles and ¼ cup gravy):
Calories: 315, **Calories from Fat:** 29%, **Total Fat:** 10g,
Saturated Fat: 3g, **Cholesterol:** 67mg, **Sodium:** 296mg,
Carbohydrate: 30g, **Dietary Fiber:** 2g, **Protein:** 25g

Dietary Exchanges: 1½ Starch, 1 Vegetable, 2½ Lean Meat

Grilled Flank Steak with Horseradish Sauce

1 beef flank steak (about 1 pound)
2 tablespoons reduced-sodium soy sauce
1 tablespoon red wine vinegar
2 cloves garlic, minced
½ teaspoon black pepper
1 cup fat-free sour cream
1 tablespoon prepared horseradish
1 tablespoon Dijon mustard
¼ cup finely chopped fresh parsley
½ teaspoon salt
6 sourdough rolls (2 ounces each), split
6 romaine lettuce leaves

1. Place flank steak in large resealable food storage bag. Add soy sauce, vinegar, garlic and pepper. Close bag securely; turn to coat. Marinate in refrigerator at least 1 hour.

2. Prepare grill for direct cooking. Drain steak; discard marinade. Grill steak over medium heat, uncovered, 17 to 21 minutes for medium rare to medium or until desired doneness, turning once. Remove from grill. Cover with foil; let stand 15 minutes. Thinly slice steak across the grain.

3. Combine sour cream, horseradish, mustard, parsley and salt in small bowl until well blended. Spread rolls with horseradish sauce; layer with sliced steak and lettuce.

Makes 6 servings

Nutrients per Serving (1 sandwich [1 roll with 2 ounces cooked beef, 3 tablespoons plus 1 teaspoon horseradish sauce and 1 lettuce leaf]):
Calories: 307, **Calories from Fat:** 27%, **Total Fat:** 9g,
Saturated Fat: 3g, **Cholesterol:** 32mg, **Sodium:** 600mg,
Carbohydrate: 29g, **Dietary Fiber:** 1g, **Protein:** 24g

Dietary Exchanges: 2 Starch, 3 Lean Meat

GUEST CH

CHECK NUMBER

4948

SERVER

3

TABLE

4

Szechwan Pork Stir-Fry over Spinach

2 teaspoons sesame oil, divided
¾ cup matchstick-size carrot strips
8 ounces pork tenderloin, thinly sliced, slices halved
3 cloves garlic, minced
2 teaspoons minced bottled or fresh ginger
¼ to ½ teaspoon red pepper flakes
1 tablespoon reduced-sodium soy sauce
1 tablespoon mirin* or dry sherry
2 teaspoons cornstarch
8 ounces baby spinach
2 teaspoons sesame seeds, toasted

*Mirin, a sweet wine made from rice, is an essential flavoring in Japanese cuisine. It is available in Asian markets and the Asian or gourmet section of some supermarkets.

1. Heat 1 teaspoon oil in large nonstick skillet over medium-high heat. Add carrot strips. Cook 3 minutes, stirring occasionally. Add pork, garlic, ginger and pepper flakes to taste. Stir-fry 3 minutes or until pork is no longer pink. Combine soy sauce, mirin and cornstarch in small bowl. Add to pork mixture. Stir-fry 1 minute or until sauce thickens.

2. Heat remaining 1 teaspoon oil in medium saucepan over medium-high heat. Add spinach. Cover and cook 1 minute. Uncover and turn spinach with tongs. Cover and cook until spinach is barely wilted, about 1 minute. Transfer spinach to 2 serving plates. Spoon pork mixture over spinach. Top with sesame seeds. *Makes 2 servings*

Nutrients per Serving (½ of total recipe):
Calories: 256, **Calories from Fat:** 35%, **Total Fat:** 10g, **Saturated Fat:** 2g, **Cholesterol:** 73mg, **Sodium:** 466mg, **Carbohydrate:** 11g, **Dietary Fiber:** 3g, **Protein:** 29g

Dietary Exchanges: 2 Vegetable, 3½ Lean Meat

Yankee Pot Roast and Vegetables

1 beef chuck pot roast (2½ pounds), trimmed of visible fat and cut into pieces
Salt and black pepper (optional)
3 unpeeled medium baking potatoes (about 1 pound), cut into quarters
2 large carrots, cut into ¾-inch slices
2 stalks celery, cut into ¾-inch slices
1 medium onion, sliced
1 large parsnip, cut into ¾-inch slices
2 bay leaves
1 teaspoon dried rosemary
½ teaspoon dried thyme
½ cup reduced-sodium beef broth

SLOW COOKER DIRECTIONS

1. Sprinkle beef with salt and pepper, if desired.

2. Combine vegetables, bay leaves, rosemary and thyme in slow cooker. Place beef over vegetables. Pour broth over beef. Cover; cook on LOW 8½ to 9 hours or until beef is fork-tender.

3. Transfer beef to serving platter. Arrange vegetables around beef. Remove and discard bay leaves.   *Makes 10 servings*

Note: To make gravy, ladle the juices into a 2-cup measure; let stand 5 minutes. Skim off and discard fat. Measure remaining juices and heat to a boil in small saucepan. For each cup of juice, mix 2 tablespoons of flour with ¼ cup of cold water until smooth. Stir mixture into boiling juices, stirring constantly 1 minute or until thickened.

Nutrients per Serving (¹⁄₁₀ of total recipe [without salt and pepper seasoning]):
Calories: 270, **Calories from Fat:** 33%, **Total Fat:** 10g, **Saturated Fat:** 4g, **Cholesterol:** 75mg, **Sodium:** 99mg, **Carbohydrate:** 15g, **Dietary Fiber:** 3g, **Protein:** 28g

Dietary Exchanges: 1 Starch, 3½ Lean Meat

Potato and Pork Frittata

12 ounces (about 3 cups) frozen hash brown potatoes
1 teaspoon Cajun seasoning
4 egg whites
2 eggs
¼ cup low-fat (1%) milk
1 teaspoon dry mustard
¼ teaspoon black pepper
10 ounces (about 3 cups) frozen stir-fry vegetable blend
⅓ cup water
¾ cup chopped cooked lean pork
½ cup (2 ounces) reduced-fat shredded Cheddar cheese

1. Preheat oven to 400°F. Spray baking sheet with nonstick cooking spray. Spread potatoes on baking sheet; sprinkle with Cajun seasoning. Bake 15 minutes or until hot. Remove from oven. *Reduce oven temperature to 350°F.*

2. Beat egg whites, eggs, milk, mustard and pepper in small bowl. Place vegetables and water in medium ovenproof nonstick skillet. Cook over medium heat 5 minutes or until vegetables are crisp-tender; drain.

3. Add pork and potatoes to vegetables in skillet; stir lightly. Add egg mixture. Sprinkle with cheese. Cook over medium-low heat 5 minutes. Place skillet in 350°F oven and bake 5 minutes or until egg mixture is set and cheese is melted. Cut into 4 wedges to serve. *Makes 4 servings*

Nutrients per Serving (1 frittata wedge [¼ of total recipe]):
Calories: 268, **Calories from Fat:** 37%, **Total Fat:** 11g,
Saturated Fat: 5g, **Cholesterol:** 145mg, **Sodium:** 258mg,
Carbohydrate: 20g, **Dietary Fiber:** 2g, **Protein:** 22g

Dietary Exchanges: 1½ Starch, 2 Lean Meat, 1 Fat

chicken

Autumn Pasta

   **1 boneless skinless chicken breast (about ¼ pound),
     cut into ½-inch cubes
8 brussels sprouts, trimmed and halved
1 large fennel bulb, trimmed, quartered and sliced
     (1½ to 2 cups)
2 medium tomatoes, chopped
¼ cup lemon juice
1 tablespoon olive oil
1 teaspoon bottled minced garlic
   Nonstick cooking spray
1 cup cooked whole grain rotini pasta
⅛ cup shredded Parmesan cheese**

1. Combine chicken, brussels sprouts, fennel, tomatoes, lemon juice, olive oil and garlic in large mixing bowl.

2. Lightly coat large skillet with cooking spray; heat over medium heat. Add chicken mixture; cook, covered, 15 minutes or until chicken is done and vegetables are tender.

3. Toss pasta into skillet with chicken mixture and heat through. Sprinkle with cheese before serving.

Makes 2 servings

Nutrients per Serving (½ of total recipe):
Calories: 315, **Calories from Fat:** 26%, **Total Fat:** 10g,
Saturated Fat: 2g, **Cholesterol:** 37mg, **Sodium:** 168mg,
Carbohydrate: 38g, **Dietary Fiber:** 9g, **Protein:** 23g

Dietary Exchanges: 1½ Starch, 3 Vegetable, 2 Lean Meat, ½ Fat

Autumn Pasta

Double-Quick Mozzarella Chicken

4 boneless skinless chicken breasts (about ¼ pound each)
½ medium lemon or lime
1 teaspoon ground cumin
¼ teaspoon salt
¾ cup (3 ounces) shredded reduced-fat mozzarella cheese
½ (10-ounce) can Mexican-style diced tomatoes with green chiles,* drained
2 tablespoons chopped fresh cilantro (optional)

Reserve remaining tomatoes for future use, if desired.

1. Preheat oven to 400°F. Coat baking sheet with nonstick cooking spray. Arrange chicken breasts on baking sheet about 2 inches apart. Squeeze lemon over chicken; sprinkle with cumin and salt. Bake 20 minutes.

2. Sprinkle cheese evenly over chicken; bake an additional 5 minutes or until chicken is no longer pink in center. Transfer chicken to serving platter. Spoon about 3 tablespoons diced tomatoes over each chicken breast. Garnish with cilantro.

Makes 4 servings

Nutrients per Serving (1 breast topped with cheese and tomatoes):
Calories: 197, **Calories from Fat:** 27%, **Total Fat:** 6g,
Saturated Fat: 2g, **Cholesterol:** 70mg, **Sodium:** 490mg,
Carbohydrate: 4g, **Dietary Fiber:** 1g, **Protein:** 29g

Dietary Exchanges: ½ Vegetable, 3½ Lean Meat

Chicken Chow Mein

1 pound boneless skinless chicken breasts, cut into
   thin strips
2 cloves garlic, minced
1 teaspoon vegetable oil, divided
2 tablespoons dry sherry
2 tablespoons reduced-sodium soy sauce
6 ounces (about 2 cups) fresh snow peas, cut in half
   crosswise *or* 1 package (6 ounces) frozen snow
   peas, thawed
3 large green onions, cut diagonally into 1-inch pieces
4 ounces uncooked Chinese egg noodles or
   vermicelli, cooked and drained
1 teaspoon dark sesame oil (optional)
   Cherry tomatoes (optional)
   Fresh herbs (optional)

1. Toss chicken and garlic in medium bowl.

2. Heat ½ teaspoon vegetable oil in wok or large nonstick
skillet over medium-high heat. Add chicken mixture; stir-fry
3 minutes or until chicken is no longer pink. Transfer to medium
bowl; toss with sherry and soy sauce.

3. Heat remaining ½ teaspoon vegetable oil in wok. Add snow
peas; stir-fry 2 minutes for fresh or 1 minute for frozen snow
peas. Add green onions; stir-fry 30 seconds. Add chicken
mixture; stir-fry 1 minute.

4. Add noodles to wok; stir-fry 2 minutes or until heated
through. Stir in sesame oil, if desired. Garnish with cherry
tomatoes and fresh herbs.   *Makes 4 servings*

Nutrients per Serving (1 cup):
Calories: 252, **Calories from Fat:** 10%, **Total Fat:** 3g,
Saturated Fat: 1g, **Cholesterol:** 66mg, **Sodium:** 461mg,
Carbohydrate: 22g, **Dietary Fiber:** 2g, **Protein:** 31g

Dietary Exchanges: 1 Starch, 1 Vegetable, 3 Lean Meat

Family-Style Creamy Chicken and Noodles

8 ounces uncooked yolk-free wide egg noodles
4 cups water
1 pound boneless skinless chicken breasts
1½ cups chopped onions
¾ cup chopped celery
½ teaspoon salt
½ teaspoon dried thyme
1 bay leaf
⅛ teaspoon white pepper
1 can (10¾ ounces) condensed cream of chicken soup, undiluted
½ cup buttermilk
Chopped fresh parsley (optional)

1. Cook pasta according to package directions. Drain; set aside.

2. Meanwhile, bring water to a boil in Dutch oven over high heat. Add chicken breasts, onions, celery, salt, thyme, bay leaf and white pepper. Return to a boil. Reduce heat to low; simmer, uncovered, 35 minutes. Remove chicken; cut into ½-inch pieces. Set aside.

3. Increase heat to high. Return liquid in Dutch oven to a boil. Continue cooking until liquid and vegetables have reduced to 1 cup. Remove from heat; discard bay leaf. Whisk in soup and buttermilk until well blended. Add chicken pieces and pasta; toss to blend. Garnish with parsley.   *Makes 6 servings*

Nutrients per Serving (⅙ of total recipe):
Calories: 289, **Calories from Fat:** 22%, **Total Fat:** 7g,
Saturated Fat: 2g, **Cholesterol:** 74mg, **Sodium:** 669mg,
Carbohydrate: 33g, **Dietary Fiber:** 2g, **Protein:** 22g

Dietary Exchanges: 2 Starch, ½ Vegetable, 2 Lean Meat

Grilled Chicken with Extra Spicy Corn and Black Beans

3 tablespoons MRS. DASH® Extra Spicy Seasoning Blend, divided
1 cup canned black beans, drained and rinsed
1 cup frozen yellow corn, thawed, cooked and cooled
1 medium red bell pepper, seeded and chopped (optional)
¼ cup finely chopped red onion
½ cup finely chopped fresh cilantro
2 tablespoons fresh lime juice
4 boneless skinless chicken breasts

At least one hour before grilling chicken, to prepare Salsa, mix 2 tablespoons Mrs. Dash® Extra Spicy Seasoning, black beans, yellow corn, pepper (if using), red onion, cilantro and fresh lime juice until well blended. Set aside, stirring once or twice. To prepare Chicken, preheat grill to medium high. Place 1 tablespoon Mrs. Dash® Extra Spicy Seasoning in a plastic bag. Place chicken in the bag and shake until well coated. Place on grill and cook 5 minutes. Turn and cook additional 5 minutes, or until juices run clear when skewer is inserted. Serve hot with salsa on the side. *Makes 4 servings*

Preparation Time: 10 minutes
Cooking Time: 12 minutes

Nutrients per Serving (½ cup plus 1 tablespoon salsa per serving):
Calories: 220, **Calories from Fat:** 7%, **Total Fat:** 2g,
Saturated Fat: <1g, **Cholesterol:** 66mg, **Sodium:** 262mg,
Carbohydrate: 20g, **Dietary Fiber:** 4g, **Protein:** 31g

Dietary Exchanges: 1 Starch, 1 Vegetable, 3 Lean Meat

Festive Skillet Fajitas

1½ pounds boneless, skinless chicken breasts, cut into
    ½-inch strips
1 medium onion, cut into thin wedges
2 cloves garlic, minced
1 tablespoon vegetable oil
½ teaspoon ground cumin
1 can (14½ ounces) DEL MONTE® Petite Cut Diced
    Tomatoes with Zesty Jalapeños
1 can (7 ounces) whole green chiles, drained and cut
    into strips
8 flour tortillas, warmed

1. Brown chicken with onion and garlic in oil in large skillet over medium-high heat.

2. Stir in cumin, tomatoes and chiles; heat through.

3. Fill warmed tortillas with chicken mixture. Garnish with sour cream, avocado or guacamole, cilantro and lime wedges, if desired. Serve immediately. *Make 8 servings*

Prep Time: 10 minutes
Cook Time: 10 minutes

Nutrients per Serving (1 fajita [without garnishes]):
Calories: 334, **Calories from Fat:** 24%, **Total Fat:** 9g,
Saturated Fat: 2g, **Cholesterol:** 69mg, **Sodium:** 233mg,
Carbohydrate: 32g, **Dietary Fiber:** 4g, **Protein:** 30g

Dietary Exchanges: 1 Starch, 3 Vegetable, 3 Lean Meat

Creole Vegetables and Chicken

Nonstick cooking spray
1 can (about 14 ounces) no-salt-added diced
  tomatoes
8 ounces frozen cut okra
2 cups chopped green bell peppers
1 cup chopped yellow onions
1 cup fat-free reduced-sodium chicken broth
¾ cup sliced celery
2 teaspoons Worcestershire sauce
1 teaspoon dried thyme
1 bay leaf
1 pound chicken tenders, cut into bite-size pieces
1 tablespoon olive oil
1½ teaspoons sugar substitute
¾ teaspoon Creole seasoning
  Hot pepper sauce (optional)
¼ cup chopped fresh parsley

SLOW COOKER DIRECTIONS

1. Coat 3½- to 4-quart slow cooker with cooking spray.
Add tomatoes, okra, bell peppers, onions, broth, celery,
Worcestershire sauce, thyme and bay leaf. Cover; cook on
LOW 9 hours or on HIGH 4½ hours.

2. Coat 10-inch nonstick skillet with cooking spray. Add
chicken; cook, stirring frequently, over medium-high heat
6 minutes or until lightly browned. Add to slow cooker with
remaining ingredients except parsley. Increase slow cooker
temperature to HIGH. Cook on HIGH 15 minutes; add parsley.

Makes 4 servings

Nutrients per Serving (1½ cups):
Calories: 190, **Calories from Fat:** 23%, **Total Fat:** 6g,
Saturated Fat: 1g, **Cholesterol:** 42mg, **Sodium:** 174mg,
Carbohydrate: 18g, **Dietary Fiber:** 6g, **Protein:** 20g

Dietary Exchanges: 3½ Vegetable, 2½ Lean Meat

Sassy Chicken & Peppers

2 teaspoons Mexican seasoning*
2 boneless skinless chicken breasts (about ¼ pound each)
2 teaspoons vegetable oil
1 small red onion, sliced
½ medium red bell pepper, cut into thin strips
½ medium yellow or green bell pepper, cut into thin strips
¼ cup chunky salsa or chipotle salsa
1 tablespoon lime juice
Lime wedges (optional)

*If Mexican seasoning is not available, substitute 1 teaspoon chili powder, ½ teaspoon ground cumin, ½ teaspoon salt and ⅛ teaspoon ground red pepper.

1. Sprinkle seasoning over both sides of chicken; set aside.

2. Heat oil in large nonstick skillet over medium heat. Add onion; cook 3 minutes, stirring occasionally.

3. Add bell pepper; cook 3 minutes, stirring occasionally. Stir salsa and lime juice into vegetables.

4. Push vegetables to edge of skillet. Add chicken to skillet. Cook 5 minutes; turn. Continue to cook 4 minutes or until chicken is no longer pink in center and vegetables are tender.

5. Transfer chicken to serving plates; top with vegetable mixture. Garnish with lime wedges.   *Makes 2 servings*

Nutrients per Serving (½ of total recipe):
Calories: 224, **Calories from Fat:** 31%, **Total Fat:** 8g,
Saturated Fat: 1g, **Cholesterol:** 69mg, **Sodium:** 813mg,
Carbohydrate: 11g, **Dietary Fiber:** 3g, **Protein:** 27g

Dietary Exchanges: 2 Vegetable, 3 Lean Meat

Sassy Chicken & Peppers

Chicken & Spinach Quesadillas with Pico de Gallo

2 cups chopped seeded tomatoes, divided
1 cup chopped green onions, divided
½ cup chopped fresh cilantro
1 tablespoons minced jalapeño pepper*
1 tablespoon fresh lime juice
   Nonstick cooking spray
10 (8-inch) fat-free flour tortillas
1 cup packed chopped stemmed spinach
1 cup shredded cooked boneless skinless chicken breast
¾ cup shredded reduced-fat Cheddar cheese

*Jalapeño peppers can sting and irritate the skin, so wear rubber gloves when handling peppers and do not touch your eyes.

1. For Pico de Gallo, mix 1½ cups tomatoes, ¾ cup green onions, cilantro, jalapeño and lime juice in medium bowl.

2. Spray large nonstick skillet with cooking spray. Heat over medium heat. Sprinkle tortilla with water; place in skillet. Cook 20 to 30 seconds or until hot, turning once. Repeat with remaining tortillas.

3. Divide remaining ½ cup tomatoes, ¼ cup green onions, spinach and chicken among 5 tortillas; sprinkle with cheese. Top with remaining 5 tortillas.

4. Cook quesadillas, 1 at a time, over medium heat 2 minutes per side or until cheese is melted. Cut each quesadilla into 4 wedges and serve with Pico de Gallo.   *Makes 5 servings*

Nutrients per Serving (1 quesadilla with ½ cup plus 1½ teaspoons pico de gallo):
Calories: 240, **Calories from Fat:** 18%, **Total Fat:** 5g,
Saturated Fat: 5g, **Cholesterol:** 34mg, **Sodium:** 540mg,
Carbohydrate: 32g, **Dietary Fiber:** 14g, **Protein:** 18g

Dietary Exchanges: 2 Starch, 1½ Lean Meat

Chicken & Spinach Quesadillas
with Pico de Gallo

Grilled Chicken Adobo

½ **cup chopped onion**
⅓ **cup lime juice**
6 **cloves garlic, coarsely chopped**
1 **teaspoon ground cumin**
1 **teaspoon dried oregano**
½ **teaspoon dried thyme**
¼ **teaspoon ground red pepper**
6 **boneless skinless chicken breasts (about ¼ pound**
   each)
3 **tablespoons chopped fresh cilantro (optional)**

1. Combine onion, lime juice and garlic in food processor. Process until onion is finely minced. Transfer to resealable food storage bag. Add cumin, oregano, thyme and red pepper; knead bag until blended. Place chicken in bag; press out air and seal. Turn to coat chicken with marinade. Refrigerate 30 minutes or up to 4 hours.

2. Spray grid with nonstick cooking spray. Prepare grill for direct cooking. Remove chicken from marinade; discard marinade. Place chicken on prepared grid 3 to 4 inches from medium-hot coals. Grill 5 to 7 minutes on each side or until chicken is no longer pink in center. Transfer to clean serving platter and garnish with cilantro.   *Makes 6 servings*

Nutrients per Serving (1 grilled chicken breast):
Calories: 139, **Calories from Fat:** 19%, **Total Fat:** 3g,
Saturated Fat: <1g, **Cholesterol:** 69mg, **Sodium:** 61mg,
Carbohydrate: 1g, **Dietary Fiber:** <1g, **Protein:** 25g

Dietary Exchanges: 3 Lean Meat

Grilled Chicken Adobo

fish
& shellfish

Beijing Fillet of Sole

2 tablespoons reduced-sodium soy sauce
2 teaspoons dark sesame oil
4 sole fillets (about 6 ounces each)
1¼ cups shredded cabbage or coleslaw mix
½ cup crushed chow mein noodles
1 egg white, lightly beaten
2 teaspoons sesame seeds

1. Preheat oven to 350°F. Combine soy sauce and oil in small bowl. Place sole in shallow dish. Lightly brush both sides of sole with soy sauce mixture.

2. Combine cabbage, noodles, egg white and remaining soy sauce mixture in medium bowl. Spoon evenly down center of each fillet. Roll up fillets. Place seam side down in shallow foil-lined baking pan.

3. Sprinkle rolls with sesame seeds. Bake 25 to 30 minutes or until fish flakes when tested with fork.   *Makes 4 servings*

Nutrients per Serving (1 roll):
Calories: 252, **Calories from Fat:** 29%, **Total Fat:** 8g,
Saturated Fat: 1g, **Cholesterol:** 80mg, **Sodium:** 435mg,
Carbohydrate: 6g, **Dietary Fiber:** <1g, **Protein:** 34g

Dietary Exchanges: 1½ Vegetable, 4 Lean Meat

fish & shellfish

Savoy Shrimp

1 pound large raw shrimp (about 20), peeled and
    deveined, tails on
½ teaspoon Chinese five-spice powder*
2 tablespoons dark sesame oil
4 cups sliced savoy or napa cabbage
1 cup snow peas, trimmed
1 tablespoon diced candied ginger (optional)
1 tablespoon reduced-sodium soy sauce
1 teaspoon red pepper flakes
½ teaspoon ground ginger
    Juice of 1 lime
¼ cup chopped fresh cilantro (optional)

*Chinese five-spice powder is a blend of cinnamon, cloves, fennel seed, anise
and Szechuan peppercorns. It is available in most supermarkets and at Asian
grocery stores.*

1. Place shrimp in colander and rinse well; drain. Toss with
Chinese five-spice powder. Set aside.

2. Heat oil in 12-inch nonstick skillet over medium heat. Add
cabbage, snow peas, candied ginger, if desired, soy sauce,
red pepper flakes and ground ginger. Cook, stirring often, until
cabbage is tender.

3. Add shrimp and lime juice; stir. Cover skillet and reduce heat
to low. Heat for 3 minutes or until shrimp are pink and opaque.
Garnish with cilantro. *Makes 4 servings*

Nutrients per Serving (5 shrimp with 1 cup vegetables):
Calories: 234, **Calories from Fat:** 37%, **Total Fat:** 9g,
Saturated Fat: 1g, **Cholesterol:** 172mg, **Sodium:** 318mg,
Carbohydrate: 12g, **Dietary Fiber:** 3g, **Protein:** 25g

Dietary Exchanges: 2 Vegetable, 3 Lean Meat

Savoy Shrimp

Salmon-Potato Cakes with Mustard Tartar Sauce

3 unpeeled small red potatoes (about 8 ounces)
1 cup cooked flaked salmon
1 egg white
2 green onions, chopped
1 tablespoon chopped fresh parsley
½ teaspoon Cajun or Creole seasoning mix
1 teaspoon olive or canola oil
MUSTARD TARTAR SAUCE
1 tablespoon reduced-fat mayonnaise
1 tablespoon plain fat-free yogurt or fat-free sour cream
2 teaspoons coarse grain mustard
1 tablespoon chopped fresh parsley
1 tablespoon chopped dill pickle
1 teaspoon lemon juice

1. Halve potatoes; place in small saucepan with ½ cup water. Bring to a boil. Reduce heat; simmer 15 minutes or until potatoes are tender. Drain; mash potatoes with fork.

2. Combine mashed potatoes, salmon, egg white, green onions, parsley and seasoning mix in medium bowl.

3. Heat oil in nonstick skillet over medium heat. Turn ½ cup salmon mixture out into skillet; flatten slightly. Repeat for second cake. Cook 7 minutes or until browned, turning once. Meanwhile, combine all sauce ingredients in small bowl. Serve cakes with sauce. *Makes 2 servings*

Nutrients per Serving (1 cake with 2 tablespoons sauce):
Calories: 276, **Calories from Fat:** 37%, **Total Fat:** 11g, **Saturated Fat:** 2g, **Cholesterol:** 52mg, **Sodium:** 300mg, **Carbohydrate:** 24g, **Dietary Fiber:** 2g, **Protein:** 19g

Dietary Exchanges: 1½ Starch, 2 Lean Meat, 1 Fat

Salmon-Potato Cakes with
Mustard Tartar Sauce

Southwest Roasted Salmon & Corn

2 medium ears fresh corn, unhusked
1 salmon fillet (about 6 ounces), cut in half
1 tablespoon plus 1 teaspoon lime juice, divided
1 clove garlic, minced
½ teaspoon chili powder
¼ teaspoon *each* ground cumin and dried oregano
⅛ teaspoon salt, divided
⅛ teaspoon black pepper
2 teaspoons margarine, melted
2 teaspoons minced fresh cilantro

1. Preheat oven to 400°F. Spray shallow 1-quart baking dish with nonstick cooking spray.

2. Pull back corn husks, leaving attached. Discard silk. Bring husks back up over each ear. Soak corn in cold water 20 minutes.

3. Place salmon, skin side down, in prepared dish. Pour 1 tablespoon lime juice over fillets. Marinate at room temperature 15 minutes.

4. Combine garlic, chili powder, cumin, oregano, half of salt and pepper in small bowl. Pat salmon lightly with paper towel. Rub garlic mixture on salmon.

5. Place corn on one side of oven rack. Roast 10 minutes; turn.

6. Place salmon in baking dish on other side of oven rack. Roast 15 minutes or until salmon begins to flake when tested with fork and corn is tender.

7. Combine margarine, cilantro, remaining 1 teaspoon lime juice and remaining salt in small bowl. Remove husks from corn. Brush lime mixture over corn. Serve corn with salmon.

Makes 2 servings

Note: Corn can also be cooked in boiling water. Omit steps 2 and 5. Husk the corn and place in a large pot of boiling water. Cover; remove from heat and let stand for 10 minutes. Drain and brush with lime mixture. Serve corn with salmon.

Nutrients per Serving (1 salmon fillet half with 1 corn ear):
Calories: 186, **Calories from Fat:** 29%, **Total Fat:** 6g,
Saturated Fat: 1g, **Cholesterol:** 43mg, **Sodium:** 243mg,
Carbohydrate: 16g, **Dietary Fiber:** 2g, **Protein:** 19g

Dietary Exchanges: 1 Starch, 2 Lean Meat

Broiled Scallops with Honey-Lime Marinade

 2 tablespoons honey
 4 teaspoons lime juice
 1 tablespoon vegetable oil
 ¼ teaspoon grated lime peel
 ¼ teaspoon salt
 1 dash hot pepper sauce
 ½ pound bay, calico or sea scallops
 1 lime, cut into wedges

Combine honey, lime juice, oil, lime peel, salt and hot pepper sauce in large bowl. Rinse scallops and pat dry with paper towel; add to marinade. Marinate scallops in refrigerator, stirring occasionally, 1 hour or overnight. Preheat broiler. Arrange scallops and marinade in single layer on 2 broiler-proof pans. Broil 4 inches from heat source 4 to 7 minutes or until opaque and lightly browned. Serve with lime wedges.

Makes 2 servings

Favorite recipe from **National Honey Board**

Nutrients per Serving (½ of total recipe):
Calories: 239, **Calories from Fat:** 30%, **Total Fat:** 8g,
Saturated Fat: 1g, **Cholesterol:** 48mg, **Sodium:** 533mg,
Carbohydrate: 23g, **Dietary Fiber:** 1g, **Protein:** 21g

Dietary Exchanges: 1½ Fruit, 3 Lean Meat

Skillet Fish with Lemon Tarragon "Butter"

2 teaspoons reduced-fat margarine
4 teaspoons lemon juice, divided
½ teaspoon grated lemon peel
¼ teaspoon dried tarragon
¼ teaspoon prepared mustard
⅛ teaspoon salt
Nonstick cooking spray
2 lean white fish fillets* (about ¼ pound each), rinsed and patted dry
¼ teaspoon paprika

Cod, orange roughy, flounder, haddock, halibut and sole can be used.

1. Combine margarine, 2 teaspoons lemon juice, lemon peel, tarragon, mustard and salt in small bowl. Stir until well blended; set aside.

2. Coat 12-inch nonstick skillet with cooking spray; heat over medium heat.

3. Drizzle fillets with remaining 2 teaspoons lemon juice. Sprinkle one side of each fillet with paprika. Place fillets in skillet, paprika side down; cook 3 minutes. Gently turn and cook 3 minutes longer or until fish begins to flake when tested with fork. Place fillets on serving plates; top with margarine mixture. *Makes 2 servings*

Nutrients per Serving (½ of total recipe):
Calories: 125, **Calories from Fat:** 24%, **Total Fat:** 3g,
Saturated Fat: 1g, **Cholesterol:** 60mg, **Sodium:** 291mg,
Carbohydrate: 1g, **Dietary Fiber:** <1g, **Protein:** 22g

Dietary Exchanges: 3 Lean Meat

Grilled Tuna Niçoise with Citrus Marinade

Citrus Marinade (page 150)
1 tuna steak (about 1 pound)
2 cups fresh green beans, trimmed and halved
4 cups romaine lettuce leaves, washed and torn
8 unpeeled small red potatoes, cooked and quartered
1 cup chopped seeded tomato
4 cooked egg whites, chopped
¼ cup red onion slices
2 teaspoons chopped black olives
Prepared fat-free salad dressing (optional)

1. Prepare Citrus Marinade; pour into large resealable food storage bag. Add tuna; seal bag. Marinate in refrigerator 1 hour, turning occasionally.* Drain tuna; discard marinade.

2. Spray grid with nonstick cooking spray. Prepare grill for direct cooking.

3. Place tuna on grid 4 inches from hot coals. Grill 8 to 10 minutes or until tuna begins to flake when tested with fork, turning once. (Or, place tuna on rack of broiler pan coated with nonstick cooking spray. Broil 4 inches from heat 8 to 10 minutes or until tuna begins to flake when tested with fork, turning once.) Slice tuna into ¼-inch-thick slices; set aside.

4. Bring 2 cups water to a boil in large saucepan over high heat. Add beans; cook 2 minutes. Drain; rinse with cold water and drain again.

5. Place lettuce on large serving platter. Arrange tuna, beans, potatoes, tomato, egg whites and onion on lettuce. Sprinkle with olives. Serve with fat-free salad dressing, if desired.

Makes 4 servings

*Marinate in refrigerator 1 hour for each inch of thickness.

continued on page 150

Grilled Tuna Niçoise with Citrus Marinade

Grilled Tuna Niçoise with Citrus Marinade, continued

Citrus Marinade

½ **cup fresh lime juice**
¼ **cup vegetable oil**
2 **green onions, chopped**
1 **teaspoon dried tarragon**
¼ **teaspoon garlic powder**
¼ **teaspoon black pepper**

Blend all ingredients in small bowl.

Nutrients per Serving (¼ of total recipe):
Calories: 373, **Calories from Fat:** 16%, **Total Fat:** 7g,
Saturated Fat: 1g, **Cholesterol:** 48mg, **Sodium:** 160mg,
Carbohydrate: 45g, **Dietary Fiber:** 6g, **Protein:** 35g

Dietary Exchanges: 2 Starch, 3 Vegetable, 3 Lean Meat

Tuna Melts

1 **can (12 ounces) chunk white tuna packed in water,**
    drained and flaked
1½ **cups packaged coleslaw mix**
3 **tablespoons sliced green onions**
3 **tablespoons reduced-fat mayonnaise**
1 **tablespoon Dijon mustard**
1 **teaspoon dried dill weed**
4 **English muffins, split and lightly toasted**
⅓ **cup shredded reduced-fat Cheddar cheese**

1. Preheat broiler. Combine tuna, coleslaw mix and green onions in medium bowl. Combine mayonnaise, mustard and dill weed in small bowl. Stir mayonnaise mixture into tuna mixture. Spread tuna mixture onto muffin halves. Place on broiler pan.

2. Broil 4 inches from heat 3 to 4 minutes or until heated through. Sprinkle with cheese. Broil 1 to 2 minutes or until cheese melts.   *Makes 4 servings*

Nutrients per Serving (2 melts):
Calories: 313, **Calories from Fat:** 23%, **Total Fat:** 8g,
Saturated Fat: 2g, **Cholesterol:** 43mg, **Sodium:** 882mg,
Carbohydrate: 30g, **Dietary Fiber:** 2g, **Protein:** 30g

Dietary Exchanges: 2 Starch, 3 Lean Meat

Enlightened Jambalaya

- 1 can (28 ounces) no-salt-added diced tomatoes
- 1 medium onion, chopped
- 1 medium red bell pepper, chopped
- 1 stalk celery, chopped (about ½ cup)
- 2 tablespoons minced garlic
- 2 teaspoons dried parsley flakes
- 2 teaspoons dried oregano
- 1 teaspoon hot pepper sauce
- ½ teaspoon dried thyme
- 2 pounds large raw shrimp, peeled and deveined
- 1 cup uncooked instant rice
- 1 cup fat-free reduced-sodium chicken broth

SLOW COOKER DIRECTIONS

1. Combine tomatoes, onion, bell pepper, celery, garlic, parsley, oregano, hot pepper sauce and thyme in slow cooker. Cover and cook on LOW 8 hours or on HIGH 4 hours. Stir in shrimp. Cover and cook on LOW 20 minutes.

2. Meanwhile, prepare rice according to package directions, substituting broth for water. Serve jambalaya over hot cooked rice.   *Makes 6 servings*

Nutrients per Serving (⅙ of total recipe):
Calories: 327, **Calories from Fat:** 9%, **Total Fat:** 3g,
Saturated Fat: <1g, **Cholesterol:** 234mg, **Sodium:** 335mg,
Carbohydrate: 37g, **Dietary Fiber:** 4g, **Protein:** 36g

Dietary Exchanges: 1½ Starch, 3 Vegetable, 4 Lean Meat

Broiled Caribbean Sea Bass

**6 skinless sea bass or striped bass fillets (5 to
     6 ounces each), about ½ inch thick**
⅓ cup chopped fresh cilantro
2 tablespoons olive oil
2 tablespoons lime juice
2 teaspoons hot pepper sauce
2 cloves garlic, minced
1 package (7 ounces) black bean and rice mix
Lime wedges

1. Place fish in shallow dish. Combine cilantro, oil, lime juice, pepper sauce and garlic in small bowl; pour over fish. Cover; marinate in refrigerator at least 30 minutes, but no longer than 2 hours.

2. Prepare black bean and rice mix according to package directions; keep warm.

3. Preheat broiler. Remove fish from marinade. Place fish on rack of broiler pan; drizzle with any remaining marinade. Broil 4 to 5 inches from heat 8 to 10 minutes or until fish is opaque. Serve fish with black beans and rice and lime wedges.

Makes 6 servings

Nutrients per Serving (1 sea bass fillet with ½ cup black beans and rice):
Calories: 291, **Calories from Fat:** 23%, **Total Fat:** 7g,
Saturated Fat: 1g, **Cholesterol:** 58mg, **Sodium:** 684mg,
Carbohydrate: 25g, **Dietary Fiber:** 2g, **Protein:** 31g

Dietary Exchanges: 1½ Starch, 4 Lean Meat

Scallioned Scallops

¼ **cup all-purpose flour**
½ **teaspoon dried thyme**
½ **teaspoon paprika**
¼ **teaspoon ground red pepper**
1 **pound scallops, rinsed and patted dry**
2 **teaspoons extra-virgin olive oil**
¼ **cup finely chopped green onions**
¼ **cup dry white wine or fat-free low-sodium chicken broth**
2 **tablespoons lemon juice**
2 **tablespoons reduced-fat margarine**
½ **teaspoon salt**
2 **tablespoons chopped fresh parsley**

1. Combine flour, thyme, paprika and red pepper in shallow dish; stir until well blended. Add scallops and toss until well coated. Shake off excess flour; set aside.

2. Heat oil in 12-inch nonstick skillet over medium-high heat. Add scallops; cook 2 minutes. Turn scallops; cook 2 minutes or until opaque. Transfer scallops to serving platter; sprinkle with green onions.

3. Add wine and lemon juice to skillet. Bring to a boil; boil 1 minute or until reduced slightly, scraping up browned bits from bottom and side. Remove from heat. Stir in margarine and salt until margarine is melted. Pour over scallops; sprinkle with parsley. *Makes 4 servings*

Nutrients per Serving (¼ of total recipe):
Calories: 210, **Calories from Fat:** 39%, **Total Fat:** 9g,
Saturated Fat: <1g, **Cholesterol:** 36mg, **Sodium:** 849mg,
Carbohydrate: 10g, **Dietary Fiber:** <1g, **Protein:** 19g

Dietary Exchanges: ½ Starch, 3 Lean Meat

meatless meals

Black Bean Tostadas

1 cup rinsed and drained canned black beans, mashed
2 teaspoons chili powder
Nonstick cooking spray
4 (8-inch) corn tortillas
1 cup washed torn romaine lettuce leaves
1 cup chopped seeded tomato
½ cup chopped onion
½ cup plain fat-free yogurt
2 jalapeño peppers,* seeded and finely chopped

*Jalapeño peppers can sting and irritate the skin, so wear rubber gloves when handling peppers and do not touch your eyes.

1. Combine beans and chili powder in small saucepan. Cook over medium heat 5 minutes or until heated through, stirring occasionally.

2. Spray large nonstick skillet with cooking spray. Heat over medium heat. Sprinkle tortillas with water; place in skillet, 1 at a time. Cook 20 to 30 seconds or until hot and pliable, turning once.

3. Spread bean mixture evenly over tortillas; layer with lettuce, tomato, onion, yogurt and peppers. Garnish as desired. Serve immediately. *Makes 4 servings*

Nutrients per Serving (1 tostada):
Calories: 146, **Calories from Fat:** 9%, **Total Fat:** 2g,
Saturated Fat: <1g, **Cholesterol:** 1mg, **Sodium:** 466mg,
Carbohydrate: 29g, **Dietary Fiber:** 5g, **Protein:** 9g

Dietary Exchanges: 1½ Starch, 1½ Vegetable

Black Bean Tostada

Chunky Vegetable Chili

2 tablespoons vegetable oil
1 medium onion, chopped
2 stalks celery, diced
1 carrot, diced
3 cloves garlic, minced
2 cans (about 15 ounces each) Great Northern beans,
    rinsed and drained
1½ cups water
1 cup frozen corn
1 can (6 ounces) tomato paste
1 can (4 ounces) diced mild green chiles
1 tablespoon chili powder
2 teaspoons dried oregano
1 teaspoon salt
Chopped fresh cilantro (optional)

1. Heat oil in large skillet over medium-high heat. Add onion, celery, carrot and garlic; cook 5 minutes or until vegetables are tender, stirring occasionally.

2. Stir beans, water, corn, tomato paste, chiles, chili powder, oregano and salt into skillet. Reduce heat to medium-low. Simmer 20 minutes, stirring occasionally. Garnish with cilantro.

Makes 8 servings

Nutrients per Serving (⅛ of total recipe):
Calories: 210, **Calories from Fat:** 17%, **Total Fat:** 4g,
Saturated Fat: <1g, **Cholesterol:** 0mg, **Sodium:** 753mg,
Carbohydrate: 36g, **Dietary Fiber:** 3g, **Protein:** 10g

Dietary Exchanges: 1½ Starch, 2 Vegetable, 1 Fat

Chunky Vegetable Chili

Pan-Fried Polenta with Fresh Tomato-Bean Salsa

2½ cups chopped plum tomatoes
1 cup canned white beans, rinsed and drained
¼ cup chopped fresh basil
½ teaspoon salt
½ teaspoon black pepper
2 tablespoons olive oil, divided
1 package (16 ounces) prepared polenta, sliced into ¼-inch-thick rounds
¼ cup grated Parmesan cheese
Whole basil leaves (optional)

1. Stir together tomatoes, beans, chopped basil, salt and pepper. Let stand at room temperature 15 minutes to blend flavors.

2. Heat 1 tablespoon olive oil in medium nonstick skillet over medium-high heat. Add half of polenta slices to skillet and cook about 4 minutes or until golden brown on both sides, turning once. Remove polenta from skillet. Repeat with remaining oil and polenta slices.

3. Arrange polenta on serving plates. Top with tomato-bean mixture. Sprinkle with cheese and garnish with whole basil leaves. *Makes 4 servings*

Nutrients per Serving (1 wrap):
Calories: 234, **Calories from Fat:** 21%, **Total Fat:** 6g, **Saturated Fat:** 1g, **Cholesterol:** 0mg, **Sodium:** 340mg, **Carbohydrate:** 41g, **Dietary Fiber:** 14g, **Protein:** 8g

Dietary Exchanges: 2 Starch, 2 Vegetable, 1 Fat

Pan-Fried Polenta with
Fresh Tomato-Bean Salsa

Speedy Garden Roll-Ups

Chickpea Spread (recipe follows)
4 (7-inch) flour tortillas
½ cup shredded carrot
½ cup shredded red cabbage
½ cup (2 ounces) shredded reduced-fat Cheddar
    cheese
4 red leaf lettuce leaves

1. Prepare Chickpea Spread. Spread each tortilla with ¼ cup Chickpea Spread to about ½ inch from edge. Sprinkle each tortilla with 2 tablespoons each carrot, cabbage and cheese. Top with 1 lettuce leaf.

2. Roll up tortillas jelly-roll style. Seal with additional Chickpea Spread.

3. Serve immediately or wrap tightly with plastic wrap and refrigerate up to 4 hours.   *Makes 4 servings*

Chickpea Spread

1 can (about 15 ounces) chickpeas, rinsed and drained
¼ cup fat-free cream cheese
1 tablespoon finely chopped onion
1 tablespoon chopped fresh cilantro
2 teaspoons lemon juice
2 cloves garlic
½ teaspoon sesame oil
⅛ teaspoon black pepper

Place all ingredients in food processor or blender; cover and process until smooth.   *Makes about 1 cup*

Nutrients per Serving (1 roll-up):
Calories: 280, **Calories from Fat:** 21%, **Total Fat:** 7g,
Saturated Fat: 2g, **Cholesterol:** 10mg, **Sodium:** 633mg,
Carbohydrate: 40g, **Dietary Fiber:** 7g, **Protein:** 15g

Dietary Exchanges: 2½ Starch, ½ Vegetable, 1 Lean Meat, ½ Fat

Speedy Garden Roll-Ups

Vegetable Lasagna

Tomato-Basil Sauce (page 166)
2 tablespoons olive oil
4 medium carrots, thinly sliced
3 medium zucchini, thinly sliced
6 ounces spinach leaves, washed, stemmed and torn
¼ teaspoon salt
¼ teaspoon black pepper
1 egg
3 cups ricotta cheese
½ cup plus 2 tablespoons grated Parmesan cheese,
    divided
12 uncooked lasagna noodles
1½ cups (6 ounces) shredded mozzarella cheese
1½ cups (6 ounces) shredded Monterey Jack cheese
½ cup water

1. Prepare Tomato-Basil Sauce. Preheat oven to 350°F.

2. Heat oil in large skillet over medium heat. Add carrots; cook and stir 4 minutes. Add zucchini; cook and stir 8 minutes or until crisp-tender. Add spinach; cook and stir 1 minute or until spinach is wilted. Stir in salt and pepper.

3. Beat egg in medium bowl. Stir in ricotta cheese and ½ cup Parmesan cheese.

4. Spread 1 cup Tomato-Basil Sauce in bottom of 13×9-inch baking pan; top with 4 uncooked lasagna noodles. Spoon one third of ricotta cheese mixture over noodles; carefully spread with spatula.

continued on page 166

Vegetable Lasagna, continued

5. Spoon one third of vegetable mixture over cheese. Top with 1 cup Tomato-Basil Sauce. Sprinkle with ½ cup each mozzarella and Monterey Jack cheeses. Repeat layers 2 times beginning with noodles and ending with mozzarella and Monterey Jack cheeses. Sprinkle with remaining 2 tablespoons Parmesan cheese.

6. Carefully pour water around sides of pan. Cover pan tightly with foil.

7. Bake lasagna 1 hour or until bubbly. Uncover. Let stand 10 to 15 minutes. Cut into 8 pieces to serve.

Makes 8 servings

Tomato-Basil Sauce

> 2 cans (28 ounces each) plum tomatoes
> 1 teaspoon olive oil
> 1 medium onion, chopped
> 3 cloves garlic, minced
> 1 tablespoon sugar
> 1 tablespoon dried basil
> ¼ teaspoon salt
> ¼ teaspoon black pepper

1. Drain tomatoes, reserving ½ cup juice. Seed and chop tomatoes.

2. Heat oil in large skillet over medium heat. Add onion and garlic; cook and stir 5 minutes or until tender. Stir in tomatoes, reserved juice, sugar, basil, salt and pepper.

3. Bring to a boil over high heat. Reduce heat to low. Simmer, uncovered, 25 to 30 minutes or until most of juices have evaporated.

Makes 4 cups

Nutrients per Serving (1 piece lasagna):
Calories: 273, **Calories from Fat:** 21%, **Total Fat:** 7g,
Saturated Fat: 3g, **Cholesterol:** 19mg, **Sodium:** 424mg,
Carbohydrate: 37g, **Dietary Fiber:** 6g, **Protein:** 21g

Dietary Exchanges: 1 Starch, 4 Vegetable, 2 Lean Meat

Quick Skillet Quiche

> **4 eggs**
> **⅓ cup 1% milk**
> **2 teaspoons Cajun seasoning**
> **1 cup reduced-fat Cheddar cheese, divided**
> **1 cup UNCLE BEN'S® Instant Rice**
> **1 cup chopped fresh asparagus**
> **¾ cup chopped green onions**
> **½ cup chopped red bell pepper**

1. Preheat oven to 350°F. In medium bowl, whisk eggs, milk, Cajun seasoning and ½ cup cheese. Set aside.

2. Cook rice according to package directions.

3. Meanwhile, spray medium skillet with nonstick cooking spray. Heat over medium heat until hot. Add asparagus, green onions and bell pepper. Cook and stir 5 minutes. Add rice and mix well.

4. Shape rice mixture to form crust on bottom and halfway up side of skillet. Pour egg mixture over crust. Sprinkle with remaining ½ cup cheese. Cover; cook over medium-low heat 10 minutes or until eggs are nearly set. Transfer skillet to oven and bake 5 minutes or until eggs are completely set.

Makes 6 servings

Nutrients per Serving (1 quiche wedge):
Calories: 173, **Calories from Fat:** 34%, **Total Fat:** 6g,
Saturated Fat: 3g, **Cholesterol:** 152mg, **Sodium:** 372mg,
Carbohydrate: 17g, **Dietary Fiber:** 1g, **Protein:** 11g

Dietary Exchanges: 1 Starch, 1 Vegetable, 1 Lean Meat, ½ Fat

Barley and Swiss Chard Skillet Casserole

- **1 cup water**
- **¾ cup uncooked quick-cooking barley**
- **1 cup chopped red bell pepper**
- **1 cup chopped green bell pepper**
- **⅛ teaspoon garlic powder**
- **⅛ teaspoon red pepper flakes**
- **2 cups packed coarsely chopped Swiss chard leaves***
- **1 cup rinsed and drained canned reduced-sodium navy beans**
- **1 cup quartered cherry tomatoes (sweet grape variety)**
- **¼ cup chopped fresh basil**
- **1 tablespoon olive oil**
- **2 tablespoons Italian-seasoned dry bread crumbs**

Fresh spinach or beet greens can be substituted for Swiss chard.

1. Preheat broiler.

2. Bring water to a boil in large skillet; add barley, bell peppers, garlic powder and red pepper flakes. Reduce heat; cover tightly and simmer 10 minutes or until liquid is absorbed.

3. Remove skillet from heat. Stir in chard, beans, tomatoes, basil and olive oil. Sprinkle evenly with bread crumbs. Broil, uncovered, 2 minutes or until golden brown.

Makes 4 servings

Nutrients per Serving (1¼ cups casserole):
Calories: 288, **Calories from Fat:** 18%, **Total Fat:** 6g,
Saturated Fat: <1g, **Cholesterol:** 0mg, **Sodium:** 488mg,
Carbohydrate: 45g, **Dietary Fiber:** 12g, **Protein:** 10g

Dietary Exchanges: 3 Starch, 1½ Fat

Barley and Swiss Chard Skillet Casserole

Black Beans & Rice Stuffed Poblano Peppers

2 large poblano peppers*
½ (15-ounce) can black beans, rinsed and drained
½ cup cooked brown rice
⅓ cup mild or medium chunky salsa
**⅓ cup shredded reduced-fat Cheddar cheese or
    pepper Jack cheese, divided**

Poblano peppers can sting and irritate the skin, so wear rubber gloves when handling peppers and do not touch your eyes.

1. Preheat oven to 375°F. Lightly spray shallow baking pan with olive oil cooking spray.

2. Cut thin slice from one side of each pepper. Chop pepper slices; set aside. In medium saucepan, cook remaining peppers in boiling water 6 minutes. Drain and rinse with cold water. Remove and discard seeds and membranes.

3. Stir together beans, rice, salsa, chopped pepper and ¼ cup cheese. Spoon into peppers, mounding mixture. Place peppers in prepared pan. Cover with foil. Bake 12 to 15 minutes or until heated through.

4. Sprinkle with remaining 4 teaspoons cheese. Bake 2 minutes more or until cheese melts.   *Makes 2 servings*

Nutrients per Serving (1 stuffed poblano pepper):
Calories: 236, **Calories from Fat:** 15%, **Total Fat:** 4g,
Saturated Fat: 2g, **Cholesterol:** 7mg, **Sodium:** 772mg,
Carbohydrate: 38g, **Dietary Fiber:** 5g, **Protein:** 14g

Dietary Exchanges: 2 Starch, 1 Vegetable, 1 Lean Meat

Vegetable Paella

½ cup chopped onion
1 clove garlic, minced
   Olive oil cooking spray
1 can (about 14 ounces) fat-free reduced-sodium
   vegetable or chicken broth
1 cup uncooked rice
1 cup chopped plum tomatoes
¼ cup water
½ teaspoon *each* dried oregano and chili powder
⅛ teaspoon *each* salt and turmeric
   Black pepper (optional)
1 red bell pepper, seeded and cut into short strips
1 jar (6 ounces) marinated artichoke hearts, drained
   and quartered
½ cup frozen peas
⅛ teaspoon hot pepper sauce

MICROWAVE DIRECTIONS

1. Place onion and garlic in 2-quart microwavable casserole. Spray lightly with cooking spray. Microwave on HIGH 30 seconds.

2. Add broth, rice, tomatoes, water, oregano, chili powder, salt, turmeric and black pepper, if desired. Cover with vented plastic wrap. Microwave on HIGH 5 minutes. Stir in remaining ingredients. Microwave on MEDIUM (50%) 15 to 18 minutes or until broth is absorbed and rice is tender.   *Makes 4 servings*

Note: If plum tomatoes are unavailable, substitute 1 can (about 14 ounces) diced tomatoes. Omit water.

Nutrients per Serving (¼ of total recipe):
Calories: 262, **Calories from Fat:** 15%, **Total Fat:** 4g,
Saturated Fat: <1g, **Cholesterol:** 11mg, **Sodium:** 331mg,
Carbohydrate: 49g, **Dietary Fiber:** 5g, **Protein:** 8g

Dietary Exchanges: 3 Starch, 1 Vegetable, ½ Fat

quick dinners

Seafood & Vegetable Stir-Fry

  2 teaspoons olive oil
  ½ medium red or yellow bell pepper, cut into strips
  ½ medium onion, cut into wedges
 10 snow peas, trimmed and cut diagonally into halves
  1 clove garlic, minced
  6 ounces frozen medium cooked shrimp, thawed
  2 tablespoons stir-fry sauce
  1 cup hot cooked rice

1. Heat oil in large nonstick skillet over medium-high heat. Add bell pepper, onion and snow peas; stir-fry 4 minutes. Add garlic; stir-fry 1 minute or until vegetables are crisp-tender.

2. Add shrimp and stir-fry sauce; stir-fry 1 to 2 minutes or until heated through. Serve over rice.   *Makes 2 servings*

Nutrients per Serving (½ of total recipe):
Calories: 279, **Calories from Fat:** 19%, **Total Fat:** 6g,
Saturated Fat: 1g, **Cholesterol:** 166mg, **Sodium:** 724mg,
Carbohydrate: 33g, **Dietary Fiber:** 2g, **Protein:** 22g

Dietary Exchanges: 1½ Starch, 2 Vegetable, 2 Lean Meat

Seafood & Vegetable Stir-Fry

Spicy Turkey Casserole

1 tablespoon olive oil
1 pound turkey breast cutlets, cut into ½-inch pieces
2 spicy turkey or chicken sausages (about 3 ounces each), cut into ½-inch slices
1 cup diced green bell pepper
½ cup sliced mushrooms
½ cup diced onion
1 jalapeño pepper,* seeded and minced (optional)
½ cup fat-free reduced-sodium chicken broth or water
1 can (about 14 ounces) no-salt-added diced tomatoes
1 teaspoon Italian seasoning
¼ teaspoon black pepper
½ teaspoon paprika
1 cup cooked yolk-free egg noodles
6 tablespoons grated Parmesan cheese
2 tablespoons coarse plain dry bread crumbs

Jalapeño peppers can sting and irritate the skin, so wear rubber gloves when handling peppers and do not touch your eyes.

1. Preheat oven to 350°F. Heat oil in large nonstick skillet over medium heat. Add turkey and sausages; cook and stir 2 minutes. Add bell pepper, mushrooms, onion and jalapeño pepper, if desired; cook and stir 5 minutes. Add chicken broth; cook 1 minute, scraping up any browned bits from bottom of skillet. Add tomatoes, seasonings and noodles.

2. Spoon turkey mixture into shallow 10-inch round baking dish. Sprinkle with cheese and bread crumbs. Bake 15 to 20 minutes or until mixture is hot and bread crumbs are golden brown.   *Makes 6 servings*

Nutrients per Serving (1 cup casserole):
Calories: 268, **Calories from Fat:** 23%, **Total Fat:** 6g,
Saturated Fat: 2g, **Cholesterol:** 52mg, **Sodium:** 347mg,
Carbohydrate: 23g, **Dietary Fiber:** 3g, **Protein:** 25g

Dietary Exchanges: 1 Starch, 1 Vegetable, 3 Lean Meat

Spicy Turkey Casserole

Barbecue Chicken with Corn Bread Topper

1½ pounds boneless skinless chicken breasts and thighs
1 can (about 15 ounces) red beans, rinsed and drained
1 can (8 ounces) tomato sauce
1 cup chopped green bell pepper
½ cup barbecue sauce
1 package (6 ounces) corn bread mix, plus ingredients to prepare mix

1. Cut chicken into ¾-inch cubes. Heat large nonstick skillet over medium heat. Add chicken; cook and stir 5 minutes or until cooked through.

2. Combine chicken, beans, tomato sauce, bell pepper and barbecue sauce in 8-inch microwavable ovenproof dish.

3. Preheat oven to 375°F. Loosely cover chicken mixture with plastic wrap or waxed paper. Microwave on MEDIUM-HIGH (70%) 8 minutes or until heated through, stirring after 4 minutes.

4. While chicken mixture is heating, prepare corn bread mix according to package directions. Spoon batter over chicken mixture. Bake 15 to 18 minutes or until toothpick inserted into center of corn bread layer comes out clean.

Makes 8 servings

Nutrients per Serving (⅛ of total recipe):
Calories: 324, **Calories from Fat:** 22%, **Total Fat:** 8g,
Saturated Fat: 1g, **Cholesterol:** 51mg, **Sodium:** 781mg,
Carbohydrate: 38g, **Dietary Fiber:** 6g, **Protein:** 26g

Dietary Exchanges: 2½ Starch, 2½ Lean Meat

Grilled Salmon Fillets, Asparagus and Onions

- ½ teaspoon paprika
- 6 salmon fillets (about 6 ounces each)
- ⅓ cup bottled honey-Dijon marinade or barbecue sauce
- 1 bunch (about 1 pound) asparagus spears, tough ends trimmed
- 1 large red or sweet onion, cut into ¼-inch slices
- 1 tablespoon olive oil
- ¼ teaspoon salt
- ¼ teaspoon black pepper

1. Prepare grill for direct cooking. Place salmon in shallow dish; sprinkle with paprika. Brush marinade over salmon; marinate at room temperature 15 minutes.

2. Brush asparagus and onion slices with olive oil; season with salt and pepper.

3. Place salmon, skin side down, in center of oiled grid over medium coals. Arrange asparagus spears and onion slices around salmon. Grill salmon and vegetables on covered grill 5 minutes. Turn salmon, asparagus and onion slices. Grill 5 to 6 minutes or until salmon begins to flake when tested with a fork and vegetables are crisp-tender. Separate onion slices into rings. Serve salmon with asparagus and onion.

Makes 6 servings

Prep and Cook Time: 26 minutes

Nutrients per Serving (1 salmon fillet with ¾ cup asparagus and onion mixture):
Calories: 255, **Calories from Fat:** 30%, **Total Fat:** 8g,
Saturated Fat: 1g, **Cholesterol:** 86mg, **Sodium:** 483mg,
Carbohydrate: 8g, **Dietary Fiber:** 2g, **Protein:** 35g

Dietary Exchanges: 1 Vegetable, 4 Lean Meat

Grilled Salmon Fillet, Asparagus and Onions

Turkey Sausage & Pasta Toss

8 ounces uncooked penne or gemelli pasta

1 can (about 14 ounces) no-salt-added stewed tomatoes

6 ounces turkey kielbasa or smoked turkey sausage, cut into ¼-inch slices

2 cups (1-inch) fresh asparagus pieces or broccoli florets

2 tablespoons reduced-fat pesto

2 tablespoons grated Parmesan cheese

1. Cook pasta according to package directions, omitting salt.

2. Meanwhile, heat tomatoes in medium saucepan; add turkey kielbasa. Stir in asparagus and pesto; cover and simmer about 6 minutes or until asparagus is crisp-tender.

3. Drain pasta; toss with tomato mixture and sprinkle with cheese.   *Makes 4 servings*

Prep and Cook Time: 25 minutes

Nutrients per Serving (¼ of total recipe):
Calories: 342, **Calories from Fat:** 18%, **Total Fat:** 7g, **Saturated Fat:** 2g, **Cholesterol:** 30mg, **Sodium:** 483mg, **Carbohydrate:** 53g, **Dietary Fiber:** 5g, **Protein:** 18g

Dietary Exchanges: 3 Starch, 1 Vegetable, 2 Lean Meat

tip

Turkey is naturally low in fat, making it a popular healthy alternative to pork and beef in some favorite indulgences, like bacon and sausage. You can find these turkey products in most large supermarkets.

Crispy Oven-Baked Chicken

4 boneless skinless chicken breasts (about 4 ounces each)
¾ cup GUILTLESS GOURMET® Roasted Red Pepper Salsa
Nonstick cooking spray
1 cup (3.5 ounces) crushed* GUILTLESS GOURMET® Baked Tortilla Chips (yellow corn, red corn or chili lime)
Cherry tomatoes and pineapple sage leaves (optional)

*Crush tortilla chips in the original bag or between two pieces of waxed paper with a rolling pin.

Wash chicken; pat dry with paper towels. Place chicken in shallow nonmetal pan or place in large resealable plastic food storage bag. Pour salsa over chicken. Cover with foil or seal bag; marinate in refrigerator 8 hours or overnight.

Preheat oven to 350°F. Coat baking sheet with cooking spray. Place crushed chips on waxed paper. Remove chicken from salsa, discarding salsa; roll chicken in crushed chips. Place on prepared baking sheet; bake 45 minutes or until chicken is no longer pink in center and chips are crisp. Serve hot. Garnish with tomatoes and sage, if desired.   *Makes 4 servings*

Nutrients per Serving (¼ of total recipe):
Calories: 245, **Calories from Fat:** 18%, **Total Fat:** 5g,
Saturated Fat: 1g, **Cholesterol:** 69mg, **Sodium:** 272mg,
Carbohydrate: 21g, **Dietary Fiber:** 2g, **Protein:** 27g

Dietary Exchanges: 1½ Starch, 3 Lean Meat

Pan Seared Halibut Steaks with Avocado Salsa

4 tablespoons chipotle salsa, divided
½ teaspoon salt, divided
4 small (4- to 5-ounce) *or* 2 large (8- to 10-ounce) halibut steaks, cut ¾ inch thick
½ cup diced tomato
½ ripe avocado, diced
2 tablespoons chopped fresh cilantro (optional)
Lime wedges (optional)

1. Combine 2 tablespoons salsa and ¼ teaspoon salt; spread over both sides of halibut.

2. Heat large nonstick skillet over medium heat. Add halibut; cook 4 to 5 minutes per side or until fish begins to flake when tested with fork.

3. Meanwhile, combine remaining 2 tablespoons salsa, ¼ teaspoon salt, tomato, avocado and cilantro, if desired, in small bowl. Mix well and spoon over cooked fish. Garnish with lime wedges.   *Makes 4 servings*

Nutrients per Serving (1 cooked small [or ½ cooked large] halibut steak with about 3 tablespoons Avocado Salsa):
Calories: 169, **Calories from Fat:** 36%, **Total Fat:** 7g, **Saturated Fat:** <1g, **Cholesterol:** 36mg, **Sodium:** 476mg, **Carbohydrate:** 2g, **Dietary Fiber:** 4g, **Protein:** 25g

Dietary Exchanges: 3 Lean Meat

Mediterranean Pork Pocket Sandwiches

¾ pound boneless lean top loin pork chops (¾ inch thick)

⅓ cup bottled fat-free Italian Caesar salad dressing

1 cup finely chopped seeded cucumber

⅓ cup plain fat-free yogurt

¼ cup finely chopped red onion

2 (6-inch) rounds whole wheat pita bread, cut in half

1. Preheat oven to 450°F. Spray shallow baking pan with nonstick cooking spray; set aside.

2. Cut pork into thin strips. Place in medium bowl. Drizzle with salad dressing; toss to coat.

3. Spread pork mixture in single layer in prepared baking pan. Bake 10 to 12 minutes or until meat starts to brown.

4. Meanwhile, combine cucumber, yogurt and red onion in medium bowl; toss. Using slotted spoon, spoon meat and cucumber mixture into pita halves. *Makes 4 servings*

Tip: For cold sandwiches, chill the meat and cucumber mixtures in separate containers, then fill pita halves or wrap in whole wheat tortillas.

Nutrients per Serving (1 pita half plus 5 tablespoons cucumber mixture): **Calories:** 209, **Calories from Fat:** 13%, **Total Fat:** 3g, **Saturated Fat:** 572g, **Cholesterol:** 47mg, **Sodium:** 578mg, **Carbohydrate:** 21g, **Dietary Fiber:** 3g, **Protein:** 24g

Dietary Exchanges: 1 Starch, 1 Vegetable, 2 Lean Meat

Easy Cheesy Ham and Veggie Rice Casserole

1 packet (3½ ounces) boil-in-a-bag brown rice
2 cups broccoli florets
1 cup (3 ounces) matchstick-size carrot strips
6 ounces lean reduced-sodium ham, diced
2 ounces Swiss cheese, broken into small pieces
¾ cup (3 ounces) shredded reduced-fat sharp Cheddar cheese, divided
1 tablespoon trans-fat-free reduced-calorie margarine
⅛ teaspoon ground red pepper

1. Cook rice in large saucepan according to package directions, omitting salt and fat. Remove rice packet when cooked; reserve water.

2. Add broccoli and carrots to water in saucepan. Bring to a boil; reduce heat, cover and simmer 3 minutes or until broccoli is crisp-tender.

3. Drain vegetables; return vegetables and cooked rice to saucepan; heat over medium-low heat. Add ham, Swiss, 1 ounce Cheddar, margarine and red pepper; stir gently. Sprinkle evenly with remaining Cheddar; cover and cook 3 minutes or until cheese melts. *Makes 4 servings*

Nutrients per Serving (1½ cups):
Calories: 283, **Calories from Fat:** 38%, **Total Fat:** 12g, **Saturated Fat:** 6g, **Cholesterol:** 48mg, **Sodium:** 616mg, **Carbohydrate:** 26g, **Dietary Fiber:** 2g, **Protein:** 19g

Dietary Exchanges: 1½ Starch, 1 Vegetable, 2 Lean Meat, 1 Fat

Hot Chinese Chicken Salad

8 ounces fresh or steamed Chinese egg noodles
¼ cup fat-free reduced-sodium chicken broth
2 tablespoons rice wine vinegar
2 tablespoons reduced-sodium soy sauce
1 tablespoon rice wine or dry sherry
1 teaspoon sugar
½ teaspoon red pepper flakes
1 tablespoon vegetable oil, divided
1½ cups fresh pea pods, diagonally sliced
1 cup thinly sliced green or red bell pepper
1 clove garlic, minced
1 pound boneless skinless chicken breasts, cut into
   ½-inch pieces
1 cup thinly sliced red or green cabbage
2 green onions, thinly sliced

1. Cook noodles in boiling water 4 to 5 minutes or until tender. Drain; set aside. Blend chicken broth, vinegar, soy sauce, rice wine, sugar and red pepper flakes in small bowl; set aside.

2. Heat 1 teaspoon oil in large nonstick skillet or wok. Add pea pods, bell pepper and garlic; cook 1 to 2 minutes or until vegetables are crisp-tender. Remove from skillet; set aside.

3. Heat remaining 2 teaspoons oil in skillet. Add chicken; cook 3 to 4 minutes or until chicken is cooked through. Add cabbage, cooked vegetables and noodles. Stir in sauce; toss until well blended. Cook and stir 1 to 2 minutes or until heated through. Sprinkle with green onions before serving.

Makes 6 servings

Nutrients per Serving (1⅓ cups salad):
Calories: 241, **Calories from Fat:** 14%, **Total Fat:** 4g,
Saturated Fat: 1g, **Cholesterol:** 45mg, **Sodium:** 419mg,
Carbohydrate: 27g, **Dietary Fiber:** 3g, **Protein:** 23g

Dietary Exchanges: 1½ Starch, 1 Vegetable, 2 Lean Meat

Hot Chinese Chicken Salad

Turkey-Tortilla Bake

9 (6-inch) corn tortillas
½ pound lean ground turkey
½ cup chopped onion
¾ cup mild or medium taco sauce
1 can (4 ounces) chopped mild green chiles, drained
½ cup frozen corn, thawed
½ cup (2 ounces) shredded reduced-fat Cheddar
   cheese
Sour cream (optional)

1. Preheat oven to 400°F. Place tortillas on large baking sheet, overlapping as little as possible; bake 4 minutes. Turn tortillas; continue baking 2 minutes or until crisp. Cool completely on wire rack.

2. Heat medium nonstick skillet over medium heat. Add turkey and onion. Cook and stir 5 minutes or until turkey is browned and onion is tender. Add taco sauce, chiles and corn. Reduce heat and simmer 5 minutes.

3. Break 3 tortillas and arrange over bottom of 1½-quart casserole. Spoon half of turkey mixture over tortillas; sprinkle with half of cheese. Repeat layers. Bake 10 minutes or until cheese is melted and casserole is heated through. Break remaining 3 tortillas into pieces and sprinkle over casserole. Garnish with sour cream.   *Makes 4 servings*

Prep and Cook Time: 30 minutes

Nutrients per Serving (1 wedge):
Calories: 279, **Calories from Fat:** 25%, **Total Fat:** 8g,
Saturated Fat: 2g, **Cholesterol:** 26mg, **Sodium:** 666mg,
Carbohydrate: 38g, **Dietary Fiber:** 1g, **Protein:** 17g

Dietary Exchanges: 2½ Starch, 1 Lean Meat, 1 Fat

Lighter Stuffed Peppers

1 can (10¾ ounces) condensed reduced-fat tomato
    soup, undiluted, divided
¼ cup water
8 ounces 93% lean ground turkey
1 cup cooked rice
¾ cup frozen corn, thawed
¼ cup sliced celery
¼ cup chopped red bell pepper
1 teaspoon Italian seasoning
½ teaspoon hot pepper sauce
2 green, yellow or red bell peppers, cut in half
    lengthwise and seeds removed

1. Blend ¼ cup soup and water in small bowl. Pour into 8-inch square baking dish; set aside. Brown turkey in large nonstick skillet over medium-high heat; drain well. Combine remaining soup with cooked turkey, rice, corn, celery, chopped bell pepper, Italian seasoning and hot pepper sauce in large bowl; mix well.

2. Fill pepper halves equally with turkey mixture. Place stuffed peppers on top of soup mixture in baking dish. Cover and bake at 350°F 35 to 40 minutes. To serve, place peppers in serving dish and spoon remaining sauce from baking dish over peppers. *Makes 4 servings*

Nutrients per Serving (1 stuffed bell pepper half):
Calories: 204, **Calories from Fat:** 13%, **Total Fat:** 3g,
Saturated Fat: 1g, **Cholesterol:** 22mg, **Sodium:** 326mg,
Carbohydrate: 33g, **Dietary Fiber:** 3g, **Protein:** 13g

Dietary Exchanges: 1½ Starch, 1½ Vegetable, 1 Lean Meat

desserts
contents

classic
sweets

Individual Tiramisù Cups

  4 whole ladyfingers, broken into bite-size pieces
  6 tablespoons cold strong coffee
  2 packets sugar substitute
  ½ teaspoon vanilla
  ½ cup thawed frozen fat-free whipped topping
  1½ teaspoons unsweetened cocoa powder
  1 tablespoon sliced almonds

1. Place half the ladyfinger pieces in each of two 6-ounce custard cups. Set aside.

2. Combine coffee, sugar substitute and vanilla in a small bowl. Stir until sugar substitute is dissolved. Spoon 3 tablespoons of coffee mixture over each serving of ladyfinger pieces

3. Place whipped topping in small bowl. Fold in cocoa until blended. Spoon topping evenly over ladyfingers. Cover with plastic wrap and refrigerate at least 2 hours.

4. Meanwhile, heat small skillet over medium high heat. Add almonds and toast 2 to 3 minutes or until golden, stirring constantly. Remove from heat; cool completely.

5. Sprinkle almonds over desserts just before serving.

Makes 2 servings

Nutrients per Serving (½ cup):
Calories: 148, **Calories from Fat:** 28%, **Total Fat:** 5g,
Saturated Fat: 1g, **Cholesterol:** 80mg, **Sodium:** 43mg,
Carbohydrate: 22g, **Dietary Fiber:** 1g, **Protein:** 4g

Dietary Exchanges: 1½ Starch, 1 Fat

Chocolate Flan

2 eggs, lightly beaten
24 packets NatraTaste® Brand Sugar Substitute
2 heaping tablespoons unsweetened cocoa powder
1 tablespoon cornstarch
1 teaspoon almond extract
1 (15-ounce) can evaporated skim milk
1 cup fat-free milk

1. Preheat oven to 350°F. Coat a 3-cup mold with nonstick cooking spray.

2. In a medium bowl, whisk together eggs, NatraTaste®, cocoa, cornstarch and almond extract until smooth. Stir in evaporated milk and fat-free milk. Pour mixture into mold. Place mold in a baking pan filled halfway with water.*

3. Bake 2 hours. Mixture will not look completely set, but will become firm upon cooling. Let cool at room temperature 1 hour, then refrigerate for several hours. To serve, invert mold onto a plate, or spoon flan from the mold.

Makes 8 servings

*Placing baking mold in water helps the flan cook evenly without cracking.

Nutrients per Serving (⅛ of total recipe):
Calories: 82, **Calories from Fat:** 17%, **Total Fat:** 2g,
Saturated Fat: 1g, **Cholesterol:** 56mg, **Sodium:** 93mg,
Carbohydrate: 13g, **Dietary Fiber:** <1g, **Protein:** 7g

Dietary Exchanges: ½ Starch, ½ Milk

Chocolate Flan

Apricot Dessert Soufflé

3 tablespoons butter
2 tablespoons all-purpose flour
1 cup no-sugar-added apricot pourable fruit*
⅓ cup finely chopped dried apricots
3 egg yolks, beaten
4 egg whites
¼ teaspoon cream of tartar
⅛ teaspoon salt

*¾ cup apricot fruit spread mixed with ¼ cup warm water can be substituted.

1. Preheat oven to 325°F. Melt butter in medium saucepan. Add flour; cook and stir until bubbly. Add pourable fruit and apricots; cook and stir 3 minutes or until thickened. Remove from heat; whisk in egg yolks. Cool to room temperature, stirring occasionally.

2. Beat egg whites, cream of tartar and salt in small bowl with electric mixer at high speed until stiff peaks form. Gently fold into apricot mixture. Spoon into 1½-quart soufflé dish. Bake 30 minutes or until puffed and golden brown.** Serve immediately. *Makes 6 servings*

**Soufflé will be soft in center. For a firmer soufflé, increase baking time to 35 minutes.

Nutrients per Serving (¾ cup soufflé):
Calories: 148, **Calories from Fat:** 52%, **Total Fat:** 9g,
Saturated Fat: 5g, **Cholesterol:** 123mg, **Sodium:** 151mg,
Carbohydrate: 14g, **Dietary Fiber:** 1g, **Protein:** 4g

Dietary Exchanges: 1 Fruit, ½ Lean Meat, 1½ Fat

Lemon Mousse Squares

1 cup graham cracker crumbs
2 tablespoons reduced-fat margarine, melted
1 packet sugar substitute *or* equivalent of 2 teaspoons sugar
⅓ cup cold water
1 envelope (¼ ounce) unflavored gelatin
2 eggs, well beaten
½ cup lemon juice
¼ cup sugar
2 teaspoon grated lemon peel
2 cups thawed frozen fat-free whipped topping
1 cup (8 ounces) lemon sugar-free fat-free yogurt

1. Spray 9-inch square baking pan with nonstick cooking spray. Stir together graham cracker crumbs, margarine and sugar substitute in small bowl. Press into bottom of pan; set aside.

2. Combine cold water and gelatin in small microwavable bowl; let stand 2 minutes. Microwave on HIGH 40 seconds to dissolve gelatin; set aside.

3. Combine eggs, lemon juice, sugar and lemon peel in top of double boiler. Cook, stirring constantly, over boiling water, about 4 minutes or until thickened. Remove from heat; stir in gelatin mixture. Refrigerate about 25 minutes or until mixture is thoroughly cooled and begins to set.

4. Gently combine lemon-gelatin mixture, whipped topping and yogurt. Pour into prepared crust. Refrigerate 1 hour or until firm. Cut into 9 squares before serving. *Makes 9 servings*

Nutrients per Serving (1 square):
Calories: 154, **Calories from Fat:** 29%, **Total Fat:** 5g, **Saturated Fat:** 1g, **Cholesterol:** 47mg, **Sodium:** 124mg, **Carbohydrate:** 24g, **Dietary Fiber:** 1g, **Protein:** 3g

Dietary Exchanges: 1½ Starch, 1 Fat

Quick Chocolate Pudding

¼ cup unsweetened cocoa powder
2 tablespoons cornstarch
1½ cups reduced-fat (2%) milk
6 to 8 packets sugar substitute *or* equivalent of
        ⅓ cup sugar
1 teaspoon vanilla
⅛ teaspoon ground cinnamon (optional)
    Assorted sugar-free candies (optional)

MICROWAVE DIRECTIONS

1. Combine cocoa powder and cornstarch in medium microwavable bowl or 1-quart glass measure. Gradually whisk in milk until well blended.

2. Microwave on HIGH 2 minutes; stir. Microwave on MEDIUM-HIGH (70%) 3 to 4½ minutes or until thickened, stirring every 1½ minutes.

3. Stir in sugar substitute, vanilla and cinnamon, if desired. Let stand at least 5 minutes before serving, stirring occasionally to prevent skin from forming. Serve warm or chilled. Garnish with candies just before serving, if desired.   *Makes 4 servings*

Nutrients per Serving (⅓ cup pudding):
Calories: 78, **Calories from Fat:** 21%, **Total Fat:** 2g,
Saturated Fat: 1g, **Cholesterol:** 7mg, **Sodium:** 56mg,
Carbohydrate: 10g, **Dietary Fiber:** <1g, **Protein:** 5g

Dietary Exchanges: ½ Milk, ½ Fat

tip

Unsweetened cocoa powder is a great way to enjoy rich chocolate flavor without a lot of fat, making it the perfect choice for delicious healthful desserts.

Rhubarb and Apple Crumble

**3 cups ¾-inch cubed and peeled Granny Smith apples
  (about 3 medium)
2½ cups ¾-inch cubed fresh red rhubarb
½ cup EQUAL® SPOONFUL*
2 tablespoons cornstarch
⅓ cup water or apple juice
1 tablespoon lemon juice
1 teaspoon grated lemon peel (optional)
¾ cup quick or old-fashioned oats, uncooked
⅓ cup EQUAL® SPOONFUL**
¼ cup raisins
¼ cup chopped nuts
2 tablespoons stick butter or margarine, melted
½ to ¾ teaspoon ground cinnamon**

*You may substitute 12 packets EQUAL® sweetener.

**You may substitute 8 packets EQUAL® sweetener.

• Combine apples, rhubarb, ½ cup Equal® Spoonful and cornstarch. Place in 1½ quart casserole dish.

• Combine water, lemon juice and lemon peel. Pour over fruit mixture. Cover and bake in preheated 400°F oven 20 to 25 minutes or until fruit is tender.

• Meanwhile, combine oats, ⅓ cup Equal® Spoonful, raisins, nuts, butter and cinnamon until well blended. Remove cover from fruit mixture. Sprinkle with oat mixture. Return to oven and bake, uncovered, 8 to 10 minutes more or until topping is crisp.

• Serve warm with frozen yogurt, ice cream or whipped topping. *Makes 6 servings*

Nutrients per Serving (⅙ of total recipe):
Calories: 177, **Calories from Fat:** 41%, **Total Fat:** 8g,
Saturated Fat: 3g, **Cholesterol:** 10mg, **Sodium:** 45mg,
Carbohydrate: 26g, **Dietary Fiber:** 4g, **Protein:** 3g

Dietary Exchanges: 1 Starch, 1 Fruit, 1½ Fat

Almond-Pumpkin Chiffon Pudding

1 envelope (¼ ounce) unflavored gelatin
1 cup 2% low-fat milk
1 cup solid pack pumpkin
½ teaspoon pumpkin pie spice
1 container (8 ounces) plain low-fat yogurt
3 egg whites
Dash salt
⅔ cup packed brown sugar
½ cup chopped roasted California Almonds, divided

Sprinkle gelatin over milk in small saucepan; let stand 5 minutes to soften. Cook and stir constantly over low heat until gelatin dissolves; remove from heat. Stir in pumpkin and pumpkin pie spice. Cool to room temperature; stir in yogurt. Refrigerate until mixture begins to thicken and gel. Beat egg whites with salt to form soft peaks. Gradually beat in brown sugar, beating to form stiff peaks; fold into pumpkin mixture. Sprinkle 1 tablespoon almonds over bottom of greased 6-cup mold. Fold remaining almonds into pumpkin mixture; spoon into mold. Refrigerate until firm. Unmold to serve.

Makes 8 servings

Favorite recipe from **Almond Board of California**

Nutrients per Serving (⅛ of total recipe):
Calories: 170, **Calories from Fat:** 27%, **Total Fat:** 5g,
Saturated Fat: 1g, **Cholesterol:** 4mg, **Sodium:** 65mg,
Carbohydrate: 25g, **Dietary Fiber:** 1g, **Protein:** 7g

Dietary Exchanges: 1½ Starch, ½ Milk, ½ Fat

Blueberry Dream Fritters

Vegetable oil
½ cup whipping cream
1 egg
1 teaspoon vanilla
1 cup self-rising flour
⅓ cup self-rising cornmeal
⅓ cup granulated sugar
1½ cups fresh blueberries
Powdered sugar

1. Heat 2 to 2½ inches oil in deep heavy saucepan over medium-high heat until oil temperature registers 375°F on deep-fry thermometer; adjust heat to maintain temperature.

2. Meanwhile, combine cream, egg and vanilla in small bowl; beat until well blended. Combine flour, cornmeal and granulated sugar in large bowl; stir into cream mixture just until moistened. Fold in blueberries.

3. Drop batter by heaping tablespoonfuls into hot oil. Fry 3 to 4 fritters at a time until golden brown, turning once. Drain on paper towels. Sprinkle with powdered sugar; serve immediately. *Makes 12 servings*

Prep and Cook Time: 20 minutes

Nutrients per Serving (1 fritter):
Calories: 110, **Calories from Fat:** 33%, **Total Fat:** 4g,
Saturated Fat: ?g, **Cholesterol:** 31mg, **Sodium:** 143mg,
Carbohydrate: 16g, **Dietary Fiber:** 1g, **Protein:** 2g

Dietary Exchanges: 1 Starch, 1 Fat

Mint Chocolate Cups

2 packages (4-serving size each) sugar-free fat-free chocolate instant pudding mix
2½ cups fat-free half-and-half
½ cup fat-free sour cream
1 teaspoon vanilla
¼ teaspoon peppermint extract
1½ cups thawed frozen fat-free whipped topping, divided
6 sugar-free peppermint patties, chopped

1. Whisk pudding mix with half-and-half in medium bowl according to package directions. Stir in sour cream, vanilla, and peppermint extract until smooth.

2. Divide half of mixture evenly among 6 parfait glasses or dessert cups. Top each with 2 tablespoons whipped topping. Top with remaining pudding mixture. Chill 1 hour or until completely cool. Garnish each serving with 2 tablespoons whipped topping and 1 chopped peppermint patty.

Makes 6 servings

Nutrients per Serving (⅔ cup pudding with ¼ cup whipped topping and 1 peppermint patty):
Calories: 166, **Calories from Fat:** <1%, **Total Fat:** <1g, **Saturated Fat:** 0g, **Cholesterol:** 15mg, **Sodium:** 541mg, **Carbohydrate:** 29g, **Dietary Fiber:** <1g, **Protein:** 6g

Dietary Exchanges: 2 Starch

cookies, brownies & bars

Chocolate Orange Meringues

  3 egg whites
  ½ teaspoon vanilla extract
  ⅛ teaspoon orange extract
  ¾ cup sugar
  ¼ cup HERSHEY'S Cocoa
  ½ teaspoon freshly grated orange peel

1. Heat oven to 300°F. Line cookie sheet with parchment paper or foil.

2. Beat egg whites, vanilla and orange extract in large bowl on high speed of mixer until soft peaks form. Gradually add sugar, beating well after each addition until stiff peaks hold their shape, sugar is dissolved and mixture is glossy. Sprinkle half of cocoa and all of orange peel over egg white mixture; gently fold in just until combined. Repeat with remaining cocoa.

3. Spoon mixture into pastry bag fitted with large star tip; pipe 1½-inch-diameter stars onto prepared cookie sheet.

4. Bake 35 to 40 minutes or until dry. Cool slightly; peel paper from cookies. Cool completely on wire rack. Store, covered, at room temperature. *Makes 5 dozen cookies*

Nutrients per Serving (3 meringues):
Calories: 35, **Calories from Fat:** 3%, **Total Fat:** <1g, **Saturated Fat:** 0g, **Cholesterol:** 0mg, **Sodium:** 8mg, **Carbohydrate:** 8g, **Dietary Fiber:** <1g, **Protein:** 1g

Dietary Exchanges: ½ Starch

Chocolate Orange Meringues

Chocolate Peanut Butter Ice Cream Sandwiches

2 tablespoons creamy peanut butter
8 chocolate wafer cookies
⅔ cup no-sugar-added vanilla ice cream, softened

1. Spread peanut butter evenly over flat sides of all cookies.

2. Spoon ice cream over peanut butter on 4 cookies. Top with remaining 4 cookies, peanut butter sides down. Press down lightly to force ice cream to edges of sandwiches.

3. Wrap each sandwich tightly in foil. Freeze at least 2 hours or up to 5 days.   *Makes 4 servings*

Nutrients per Serving (1 sandwich):
Calories: 129, **Calories from Fat:** 49%, **Total Fat:** 7g,
Saturated Fat: 3g, **Cholesterol:** 4mg, **Sodium:** 124mg,
Carbohydrate: 15g, **Dietary Fiber:** 1g, **Protein:** 4g

Dietary Exchanges: 1 Starch, 1 Fat

Peanut butter is delicious and good for you! When included in a low-fat, heart-healthy eating plan, peanut butter may help lower cholesterol and reduce the risk of heart attack.

Chocolate Peanut Butter Ice Cream Sandwiches

Chocolate Chip Cookies

⅓ cup stick butter or margarine, softened
1 egg
1 teaspoon vanilla
⅓ cup **EQUAL® SPOONFUL***
⅓ cup firmly packed light brown sugar
¾ cup all-purpose flour
½ teaspoon baking soda
¼ teaspoon salt
½ cup semi-sweet chocolate chips or mini chocolate
    chips

May substitute 8 packets EQUAL® sweetener.

• Beat butter with electric mixer until fluffy. Beat in egg and vanilla until blended. Mix in Equal® Spoonful and brown sugar until combined.

• Combine flour, baking soda and salt. Mix into butter mixture until well blended. Stir in chocolate chips.

• Drop dough by rounded teaspoonfuls onto ungreased baking sheet. Bake in preheated 350°F oven 8 to 10 minutes or until light golden color. Remove from baking sheet and cool completely on wire rack.   *Makes about 2 dozen cookies*

Nutrients per Serving (1 cookie):
Calories: 70, **Calories from Fat:** 47%, **Total Fat:** 4g,
Saturated Fat: 2g, **Cholesterol:** 16mg, **Sodium:** 74mg,
Carbohydrate: 9g, **Dietary Fiber:** <1g, **Protein:** 1g

Dietary Exchanges: ½ Starch, 1 Fat

Cinnamon Flats

1¾ cups all-purpose flour
½ cup sugar
1½ teaspoons ground cinnamon
¼ teaspoon *each* salt and ground nutmeg
½ cup (1 stick) cold margarine
3 egg whites, divided
1 teaspoon vanilla
1 teaspoon water
Sugar Glaze (recipe follows)

1. Preheat oven to 350°F. Combine flour, sugar, cinnamon, salt and nutmeg in medium bowl. Cut in margarine until mixture forms coarse crumbs. Beat in 2 egg whites and vanilla; mix with hands to form soft dough.

2. Divide dough into 6 equal pieces; place on greased 15×10-inch jelly-roll pan. Press dough evenly to edges of pan using hands; smooth top of dough. Mix remaining egg white and water in small cup; brush over dough. Lightly score dough into 2×1½-inch squares.

3. Bake 20 to 25 minutes or until lightly browned and firm when lightly touched. While still warm, cut along score lines into squares; drizzle with Sugar Glaze. Let stand 15 minutes or until glaze is firm before removing from pan.   *Makes 50 cookies*

Sugar Glaze: Combine 1½ cups powdered sugar, 2 tablespoons milk and 1 teaspoon vanilla in small bowl. If glaze is too thick, add another 1 tablespoon milk. Makes about ¾ cup.

Nutrients per Serving (1 cookie):
Calories: 48, **Calories from Fat:** 18%, **Total Fat:** 1g,
Saturated Fat: <1g, **Cholesterol:** <1mg, **Sodium:** 35mg,
Carbohydrate: 9g, **Dietary Fiber:** <1g, **Protein:** 1g

Dietary Exchanges: ½ Starch

Chocolate-Almond Meringue Puffs

2 tablespoons sugar

3 packets sugar substitute

1½ teaspoons unsweetened cocoa powder

2 egg whites, at room temperature

½ teaspoon vanilla

¼ teaspoon cream of tartar

¼ teaspoon almond extract

⅛ teaspoon salt

1½ ounces sliced almonds

3 tablespoons sugar-free seedless raspberry fruit spread

1. Preheat oven to 275°F. Combine sugar, sugar substitute and cocoa in small bowl; set aside.

2. Beat egg whites in medium bowl with electric mixer at high speed until foamy. Add vanilla, cream of tartar, almond extract and salt; beat until soft peaks form. Add sugar mixture, 1 tablespoon at a time, beating until stiff peaks form.

3. Line baking sheet with foil. Spoon 15 equal mounds of egg white mixture onto foil. Sprinkle with almonds.

4. Bake 1 hour. Turn oven off but do not open door. Leave puffs in oven 2 hours longer or until completely dry. Remove from oven; cool completely.

5. Stir fruit spread and spoon about ½ teaspoon onto each meringue just before serving. *Makes 15 servings*

Tip: Puffs are best if eaten the same day they're made. If necessary, store them in an airtight container and add the fruit topping at the time of serving.

Nutrients per Serving (1 puff):
Calories: 36, **Calories from Fat:** 36%, **Total Fat:** 1g,
Saturated Fat: <1g, **Cholesterol:** 0mg, **Sodium:** 27mg,
Carbohydrate: 5g, **Dietary Fiber:** <1g, **Protein:** 1g

Dietary Exchanges: ½ Starch

cookies, brownies & bars

Luscious Lemon Bars

2 cups all-purpose flour
1 cup (2 sticks) butter
½ cup powdered sugar, plus additional for dusting
1 tablespoon plus 1 teaspoon grated lemon peel, divided
¼ teaspoon salt
1 cup granulated sugar
3 eggs
⅓ cup fresh lemon juice

1. Preheat oven to 350°F. Grease 13×9-inch baking pan; set aside.

2. Place flour, butter, ½ cup powdered sugar, 1 teaspoon lemon peel and salt in food processor. Cover; process until mixture forms coarse crumbs. Press mixture evenly into prepared baking pan. Bake 18 to 20 minutes or until golden brown.

3. Meanwhile, beat granulated sugar, eggs, lemon juice and remaining 1 tablespoon lemon peel in medium bowl with electric mixer at medium speed until well blended.

4. Pour mixture evenly over warm crust. Return to oven; bake 18 to 20 minutes or until center is set and edges are golden brown. Remove pan to wire rack; cool completely. Dust with additional powdered sugar; cut into 2×1½-inch bars. Store tightly covered at room temperature. *Do not freeze.*

Makes 3 dozen bars

Nutrients per Serving: (1 bar):
Calories: 105, **Calories from Fat:** 51%, **Total Fat:** 6g, **Saturated Fat:** 3g, **Cholesterol:** 31mg, **Sodium:** 72mg, **Carbohydrate:** 13g, **Dietary Fiber:** <1g, **Protein:** 1g

Dietary Exchanges: 1 Starch, 1 Fat

Double Chocolate Brownies

1 cup EQUAL® SPOONFUL*
¾ cup all-purpose flour
**½ cup semi-sweet chocolate chips or mini chocolate
   chips**
6 tablespoons unsweetened cocoa
1 teaspoon baking powder
¼ teaspoon salt
6 tablespoons stick butter or margarine, softened
½ cup unsweetened applesauce
2 eggs
1 teaspoon vanilla

You may substitute 24 packets EQUAL® sweetener.

• Combine Equal®, flour, chocolate chips, cocoa, baking powder and salt. Beat butter, applesauce, eggs and vanilla until blended. Stir in combined flour mixture until blended.

• Spread batter in 8-inch square baking pan sprayed with nonstick cooking spray. Bake in preheated 350°F oven 18 to 20 minutes or until top springs back when gently touched. Cool completely in pan on wire rack.   *Makes 16 servings*

Nutrients per Serving (1 brownie [¹/₁₆ of total recipe]):
Calories: 108, **Calories from Fat:** 58%, **Total Fat:** 7g,
Saturated Fat: 4g, **Cholesterol:** 38mg, **Sodium:** 108mg,
Carbohydrate: 11g, **Dietary Fiber:** 1g, **Protein:** 2g

Dietary Exchanges: 1 Starch, 1 Fat

Peanut Butter Chocolate Bars

1 cup EQUAL® SPOONFUL*
½ cup stick butter or margarine, softened
⅓ cup firmly packed brown sugar
½ cup 2% milk
½ cup creamy peanut butter
1 egg
1 teaspoon vanilla
1 cup all-purpose flour
¾ cup quick oats, uncooked
½ teaspoon baking soda
¼ teaspoon salt
¾ cup mini semi-sweet chocolate chips

You may substitute 24 packets EQUAL® sweetener.

• Beat Equal®, butter and brown sugar until well combined. Stir in milk, peanut butter, egg and vanilla until blended. Gradually mix in combined flour, oats, baking soda and salt until blended. Stir in chocolate chips.

• Spread mixture evenly into 13×9-inch baking pan generously coated with nonstick cooking spray. Bake in preheated 350°F oven 20 to 22 minutes. Cool completely in pan on wire rack. Cut into squares; store in airtight container at room temperature.   *Makes 48 bars*

Nutrients per Serving (1 bar):
Calories: 68, **Calories from Fat:** 53%, **Total Fat:** 4g, **Saturated Fat:** 2g, **Cholesterol:** 10mg, **Sodium:** 60mg, **Carbohydrate:** 7g, **Dietary Fiber:** 1g, **Protein:** 1g

Dietary Exchanges: ½ Starch, ½ Fat

Pumpkin Polka Dot Cookies

1¼ cups **EQUAL® SPOONFUL***
½ cup (1 stick) butter or margarine, softened
3 tablespoons light molasses
1 cup canned pumpkin
1 egg
1½ teaspoons vanilla
1⅔ cups all-purpose flour
1 teaspoon baking powder
1¼ teaspoons ground cinnamon
½ teaspoon ground nutmeg
½ teaspoon ground ginger
½ teaspoon baking soda
¼ teaspoon salt
1 cup mini semi-sweet chocolate chips

May substitute 30 packets EQUAL® sweetener.

• Beat Equal®, butter and molasses until well combined. Mix in pumpkin, egg and vanilla until blended. Gradually stir in flour, baking powder, spices, baking soda and salt until well blended. Stir in chocolate chips.

• Drop by teaspoonfuls onto baking sheets sprayed with nonstick cooking spray. Bake in preheated 350°F oven 11 to 13 minutes. Remove from baking sheets and cool completely on wire rack. Store at room temperature in airtight container up to 1 week. *Makes about 4 dozen cookies*

Nutrients per Serving (1 cookie):
Calories: 63, **Calories from Fat:** 43%, **Total Fat:** 3g,
Saturated Fat: 2g, **Cholesterol:** 10mg, **Sodium:** 69mg,
Carbohydrate: 8g, **Dietary Fiber:** 1g, **Protein:** 1g

Dietary Exchanges: ½ Starch, ½ Fat

PB Berry Bars

  2 cups instant unflavored oatmeal (about 7 packets)
  ½ cup sugar-free reduced-fat peanut butter
  ½ cup mini semisweet chocolate chips, divided
  ¼ cup packed brown sugar
  ¼ cup canola oil, divided
  1 teaspoon ground cinnamon
  ¾ cup finely chopped strawberries

1. Place 12-inch skillet over medium high heat. Add oatmeal; cook and stir 6 minutes or until lightly browned and fragrant. Remove from skillet; set aside.

2. Mix peanut butter, 5 tablespoons chocolate chips, sugar, 2½ tablespoons oil and cinnamon in skillet. Cook and stir until well blended and chips are completely melted. Remove from heat. Add oats; stir until well blended. Press mixture evenly into 9-inch square baking pan using rubber spatula. Place in freezer 15 minutes to cool quickly. Sprinkle with strawberries.

3. Place small saucepan over low heat and add remaining chocolate chips and oil; stir until chips are completely melted. Drizzle melted chocolate over strawberries. Cover with foil and freeze at least 2 hours.

4. To serve, let stand 10 minutes at room temperature before cutting into squares. Store remaining pieces in freezer.

Makes 16 servings

Nutrients per Serving (1 [2¼-inch] square bar):
Calories: 158, **Calories from Fat:** 53%, **Total Fat:** 9g,
Saturated Fat: 2g, **Cholesterol:** 0mg, **Sodium:** 41mg,
Carbohydrate: 15g, **Dietary Fiber:** 2g, **Protein:** 4g

Dietary Exchanges: 1 Starch, 2 Fat

Pistachio Pinwheels

1 package (8 ounces) reduced-fat cream cheese
½ cup (1 stick) soft baking butter with canola oil
2 cups all-purpose flour
3 tablespoons apricot fruit spread
2 tablespoons sugar
¼ teaspoon ground cinnamon
½ cup finely chopped pistachio nuts, toasted*
Nonstick cooking spray

*To toast nuts, spread in single layer on baking sheet. Bake in preheated 350°F oven 8 to 10 minutes or until golden brown, stirring frequently.

1. Preheat oven to 350°F. Line cookie sheets with parchment paper. Beat softened cream cheese in large bowl with electric mixer at low speed until smooth. Add butter; beat 30 seconds at medium speed. Add flour in 3 batches, beating at low speed until blended. Divide dough into 2 portions; shape into rectangles. Wrap in plastic wrap; refrigerate 20 minutes. Mix fruit spread and 1 tablespoon water in small bowl; set aside. In separate small bowl, combine sugar and cinnamon; set aside.

2. Remove one portion dough from refrigerator. Place on lightly floured surface. Roll out dough into 12×10-inch rectangle. Spread 2 tablespoons apricot mixture on dough. Sprinkle with 1½ teaspoons cinnamon-sugar mixture, followed by ¼ cup pistachio nuts. Cut dough in half lengthwise. Roll up each half jelly-roll style, starting with long side. Repeat process with remaining dough. Cut each roll into 16 slices. Place cookies on prepared cookie sheets. Spray tops of cookies with cooking spay; sprinkle with remaining cinnamon-sugar mixture. Bake 16 minutes or until golden. Cool 2 minutes on cookie sheets. Remove to wire racks; cool completely.   *Makes 64 cookies*

Nutrients per Serving (1 cookie):
Calories: 45, **Calories from Fat:** 60%, **Total Fat:** 3g,
Saturated Fat: <1g, **Cholesterol:** 3mg, **Sodium:** 34mg,
Carbohydrate: 5g, **Dietary Fiber:** <1g, **Protein:** 1g

Dietary Exchanges: ½ Starch, ½ Fat

Pistachio Pinwheels

Double Chocolate Biscotti

¾ **cup all-purpose flour**
3 **tablespoons sugar substitute**
3 **tablespoons packed brown sugar**
2 **tablespoons unsweetened cocoa powder**
1 **teaspoon baking powder**
¼ **teaspoon salt**
2 **egg whites**
2 **tablespoons butter**
1 **tablespoon chocolate syrup**
½ **cup puffed wheat cereal**
4 **teaspoons sliced almonds**

1. Preheat oven to 350°F. Line cookie sheet with parchment paper; set aside.

2. Combine flour, sugar substitute, brown sugar, cocoa, baking powder and salt in medium bowl; set aside. Beat egg whites in small bowl with electric mixer at high speed until soft peaks form.

3. Melt butter in small saucepan. Pour into small bowl. Add chocolate syrup and egg whites; stir to combine. Stir butter mixture into flour mixture to form stiff dough. Stir in cereal.

4. Turn dough out onto cookie sheet; shape into 12×2-inch log. Press almonds onto log. Bake 20 to 25 minutes or until firm. Cool completely on wire rack.

5. *Reduce oven temperature to 300°F.* Using serrated knife, cut loaf into ½-inch-thick diagonal slices. Place slices, cut sides down, on cookie sheet. Bake biscotti 10 minutes. Turn slices; bake 10 minutes. Cool completely on wire racks.

Makes 24 servings

Nutrients per Serving (1 biscotti):
Calories: 38, **Calories from Fat:** 47%, **Total Fat:** 2g,
Saturated Fat: <1g, **Cholesterol:** 3mg, **Sodium:** 58mg,
Carbohydrate: 6g, **Dietary Fiber:** <1g, **Protein:** 1g

Dietary Exchanges: ½ Starch

Double Chocolate Biscotti

cakes & cheesecakes

Chilled Cherry Cheesecake

   4 chocolate graham crackers, crushed (1 cup crumbs)
12 ounces reduced-fat cream cheese
  8 ounces vanilla fat-free yogurt
  ¼ cup sugar
  1 teaspoon vanilla
  1 envelope (¼ ounce) unflavored gelatin
  ¼ cup cold water
  1 can (20 ounces) light cherry pie filling

1. Sprinkle cracker crumbs onto bottom of 8-inch square baking pan. Beat cream cheese, yogurt, sugar and vanilla in medium bowl with electric mixer at medium speed until smooth and creamy.

2. Sprinkle gelatin into water in small microwavable bowl; let stand 2 minutes. Microwave on HIGH 40 seconds; stir and let stand 2 minutes or until gelatin is completely dissolved.

3. Gradually beat gelatin mixture into cream cheese mixture with electric mixer at low speed until well blended. Pour into prepared pan; refrigerate until firm. Spoon cherry filling onto cheesecake. Refrigerate until ready to serve.

Makes 9 servings

Nutrients per Serving (1 piece cheesecake [⅑ of total recipe]):
Calories: 221, **Calories from Fat:** 39%, **Total Fat:** 10g,
Saturated Fat: 6g, **Cholesterol:** 29mg, **Sodium:** 226mg,
Carbohydrate: 29g, **Dietary Fiber:** 1g, **Protein:** 5g

Dietary Exchanges: 2 Starch, 1½ Fat

Pear-Ginger Upside-Down Cake

2 unpeeled Bosc pears, cored and thinly sliced
3 tablespoons fresh lemon juice
1 tablespoons butter, melted
1 tablespoons packed brown sugar
1 cup all-purpose flour
1 teaspoon *each* baking powder and ground cinnamon
¼ teaspoon baking soda
⅛ teaspoon salt
⅓ cup fat-free (skim) milk
1 egg
3 tablespoons apricot fruit spread
1 tablespoon vegetable oil
1 tablespoon minced fresh ginger

1. Preheat oven to 375°F. Spray 10-inch deep-dish pie pan with nonstick cooking spray; set aside.

2. Toss pears in lemon juice; drain. Brush butter evenly onto bottom of prepared pan; sprinkle with sugar. Arrange pears in prepared pan; bake 10 minutes.

3. Meanwhile, combine flour, baking powder, cinnamon, baking soda and salt in small bowl. Combine milk, egg, fruit spread, oil and ginger in medium bowl. Add flour mixture to milk mixture; stir until well blended. Spread batter over pears.

4. Bake 20 to 25 minutes or until golden brown and toothpick inserted into center comes out clean.

5. Cool in pan on wire rack 5 minutes. Loosen cake from side of pan. Invert cake onto large plate. Place any pears left in pan on top of cake. Serve warm. *Makes 8 servings*

Nutrients per Serving (1 slice cake [⅛ of total recipe]):
Calories: 139, **Calories from Fat:** 27%, **Total Fat:** 4g,
Saturated Fat: 1g, **Cholesterol:** 31mg, **Sodium:** 174mg,
Carbohydrate: 23g, **Dietary Fiber:** 2g, **Protein:** 3g

Dietary Exchanges: 1½ Starch, ½ Fat

Pear-Ginger Upside-Down Cake

Fresh Apple-Cinnamon Coffee Cake

1 package (17 ounces) cinnamon-swirl quick bread and coffee cake mix

¾ cup water

4 egg whites *or* ½ cup cholesterol-free egg substitute

1 teaspoon vanilla or vanilla, butter and nut flavoring

1 cup finely chopped Granny Smith apples

1. Preheat oven to 350°F. Spray 13×9-inch baking pan with nonstick cooking spray; set aside.

2. Set aside cinnamon-swirl mix. Combine quick bread mix, water, egg whites and vanilla in medium bowl; beat 50 strokes or until well blended. Spoon batter into prepared baking pan.

3. Spread apples evenly over batter; sprinkle evenly with cinnamon-swirl mix. Bake 22 minutes or until toothpick inserted into center comes out clean.

4. Remove cake to wire rack; cool 15 minutes. Cut into 16 pieces. Serve warm or at room temperature.

Makes 16 servings

Note: Flavors are at their peak when this coffee cake is served warm. To reheat, microwave on HIGH 10 to 15 seconds or until heated.

Prep Time: 10 minutes
Bake Time: 22 minutes
Cool Time: 15 minutes

Nutrients per Serving (1 piece coffee cake [$\frac{1}{16}$ of total recipe]):
Calories: 140, **Calories from Fat:** 24%, **Total Fat:** 4g,
Saturated Fat: 1g, **Cholesterol:** 0mg, **Sodium:** 131mg,
Carbohydrate: 24g, **Dietary Fiber:** <1g, **Protein:** 2g

Dietary Exchanges: 1 Starch, ½ Fruit, ½ Fat

Fresh Apple-Cinnamon Coffee Cake

Chocolate Cherry Cups

⅓ **cup all-purpose flour**
⅓ **cup sugar**
⅓ **cup unsweetened cocoa powder**
¼ **teaspoon baking powder**
¼ **teaspoon salt**
6 **ounces vanilla fat-free yogurt**
½ **teaspoon almond extract**
3 **egg whites**
36 **frozen pitted unsweetened dark sweet cherries, thawed and drained**

1. Preheat oven to 350°F. Line 12 standard (2½-inch) muffin cups with foil baking cups; set aside.

2. Combine flour, sugar, cocoa, baking powder and salt in medium bowl. Stir in yogurt and almond extract. Beat egg whites in small bowl with electric mixer at high speed until soft peaks form. Fold egg whites into batter just until blended.

3. Fill muffin cups two-thirds full. Place 3 cherries into each cup, pressing lightly into batter.

4. Bake 15 to 20 minutes until tops are puffy and edges are set. Centers will be moist.   *Makes 12 servings*

Nutrients per Serving (1 Chocolate Cherry Cup):
Calories: 62, **Calories from Fat:** 6%, **Total Fat:** <1g,
Saturated Fat: <1g, **Cholesterol:** <1mg, **Sodium:** 81mg,
Carbohydrate: 13g, **Dietary Fiber:** 1g, **Protein:** 2g

Dietary Exchanges: 1 Starch

Apricot Walnut Swirl Coffeecake

WALNUT FILLING
½ cup sugar-free apricot preserves or apricot
    spreadable fruit
¾ cup EQUAL® SPOONFUL*
4 teaspoons ground cinnamon
½ cup chopped walnuts

COFFEECAKE
2⅓ cups reduced-fat baking mix
½ cup EQUAL® SPOONFUL**
⅔ cup fat-free milk
⅓ cup fat-free sour cream
1 egg
2 tablespoons stick butter or margarine, melted
⅓ cup sugar-free apricot preserves or apricot
    spreadable fruit

*You may substitute 18 packets EQUAL® sweetener.

**You may substitute 12 packets EQUAL® sweetener.

• For Walnut Filling, mix ½ cup apricot preserves, ¾ cup Equal® Spoonful, cinnamon and walnuts in small bowl.

• For Coffeecake, combine baking mix and ½ cup Equal® Spoonful; mix in milk, sour cream, egg and butter. Spread ⅓ of batter in greased and floured 6-cup bundt pan; spoon half of Walnut Filling over batter. Repeat layers, ending with batter.

• Bake in preheated 375°F oven about 25 minutes or until coffeecake is browned on top and toothpick inserted into center comes out clean. Cool in pan 5 minutes. Invert onto wire rack; cool 5 to 10 minutes. Spoon ⅓ cup apricot preserves over top of coffeecake; serve warm.   *Makes 12 servings*

Nutrients per Serving (1 slice coffee cake [¹⁄₁₂ of total recipe]):
Calories: 189, **Calories from Fat:** 34%, **Total Fat:** 7g,
Saturated Fat: 1g, **Cholesterol:** 18mg, **Sodium:** 332mg,
Carbohydrate: 28g, **Dietary Fiber:** 1g, **Protein:** 4g

Dietary Exchanges: 2 Starch, 1 Fat

Java-Spiked Walnut Coffee Cake

2 tablespoons sugar-free fat-free mocha instant
   coffee mix
¼ teaspoon ground cinnamon
1½ cups all-purpose flour
¼ cup sugar substitute*
¼ cup sugar
1 teaspoon baking powder
½ teaspoon baking soda
⅛ teaspoon salt
1 container (6 ounces) plain fat-free yogurt
¼ cup cholesterol-free egg substitute
2 tablespoons butter, melted
1 teaspoon vanilla
¼ cup finely chopped walnuts

This recipe was tested with sucralose-based sugar substitute.

1. Preheat oven to 350°F. Spray 8-inch square baking pan with nonstick cooking spray; set aside.

2. Combine coffee mix and cinnamon in small bowl; set aside.

3. Combine flour, sugar substitute, sugar, baking powder, baking soda and salt in large bowl. Combine yogurt, egg substitute, butter and vanilla in small bowl; add to flour mixture. Stir just until moistened.

4. Spread batter into prepared pan. Sprinkle with reserved coffee mixture. Sprinkle with walnuts. Bake 30 to 35 minutes or until toothpick inserted into center comes out clean. Serve warm. Cut into 9 pieces.   *Makes 9 servings*

Nutrients per Serving (1 [2½-inch] coffee cake square):
Calories: 166, **Calories from Fat:** 28%, **Total Fat:** 5g,
Saturated Fat: 2g, **Cholesterol:** 8mg, **Sodium:** 212mg,
Carbohydrate: 25g, **Dietary Fiber:** 1g, **Protein:** 4g

Dietary Exchanges: 1½ Starch, 1 Fat

Java-Spiked Walnut Coffee Cake

Chocolate-Orange Cake Roll

⅓ cup all-purpose flour

¼ cup plus 1 tablespoon unsweetened cocoa powder, divided

¼ teaspoon baking soda

4 eggs, separated

½ teaspoon vanilla

¼ cup sugar substitute*

½ cup plus 2 tablespoons sugar, divided

½ cup orange fruit spread

*This recipe was tested with sucralose-based sugar substitute.

1. Preheat oven to 375°F. Spray 15×10×1-inch jelly-roll pan with nonstick cooking spray. Dust with flour; set aside. Combine flour, ¼ cup cocoa and baking soda in small bowl; set aside.

2. Beat egg yolks and vanilla in large bowl with electric mixer at high speed 5 to 6 minutes or until thick and pale yellow. Beat in sugar substitute and 2 tablespoons sugar.

3. Beat egg whites in another large bowl at high speed until soft peaks form. Beat in remaining ½ cup sugar until stiff peaks form; fold in egg yolk mixture. Sift flour mixture over egg mixture; fold just until blended. Spread into prepared pan. Bake 12 to 15 minutes or until top springs back when lightly touched.

4. Meanwhile, sprinkle remaining 1 tablespoon cocoa onto kitchen towel. Loosen cake from pan. Invert pan onto prepared towel. Roll up towel and cake, starting from short side. Cool on wire rack. Unroll cake; spread with orange spread. Roll up cake. *Makes 10 servings*

Nutrients per Serving (1 slice cake roll [¹⁄₁₀ of total recipe]):
Calories: 136, **Calories from Fat:** 15%, **Total Fat:** 2g,
Saturated Fat: 1g, **Cholesterol:** 85mg, **Sodium:** 60mg,
Carbohydrate: 25g, **Dietary Fiber:** 1g, **Protein:** 3g

Dietary Exchanges: 1½ Starch, ½ Fat

Chocolate-Berry Cheesecake

1 cup chocolate wafer crumbs
1 container (12 ounces) fat-free soft cream cheese
1 package (8 ounces) reduced-fat cream cheese
⅔ cup sugar
½ cup cholesterol-free egg substitute
3 tablespoons fat-free (skim) milk
1¼ teaspoons vanilla
1 cup mini semisweet chocolate chips
2 tablespoons no-sugar-added raspberry fruit spread
2 tablespoons water
2½ cups fresh strawberries, hulled and halved

1. Preheat oven to 350°F. Spray bottom of 9-inch springform pan with nonstick cooking spray; press chocolate wafer crumbs firmly onto bottom of prepared pan. Bake 10 minutes. Remove from oven; cool. *Reduce oven temperature to 325°F.*

2. Beat cheeses in large bowl with electric mixer at medium speed until well blended. Beat in sugar until well blended. Beat in egg substitute, milk and vanilla until well blended. Stir in mini chips. Pour batter into pan.

3. Bake 40 minutes or until center is set. Remove from oven; cool 10 minutes in pan on wire rack. Carefully loosen cheesecake from edge of pan. Cool completely.

4. Remove side of pan from cake. Blend fruit spread and water in medium bowl until smooth. Add strawberries; toss to coat. Arrange strawberries on top of cake. Refrigerate 1 hour before serving. *Makes 16 servings*

Nutrients per Serving (1 cheesecake slice):
Calories: 197, **Calories from Fat:** 29%, **Total Fat:** 7g,
Saturated Fat: 2g, **Cholesterol:** 7mg, **Sodium:** 290mg,
Carbohydrate: 29g, **Dietary Fiber:** <1g, **Protein:** 7g

Dietary Exchanges: 1 Starch, 1 Fruit, ½ Lean Meat, 1 Fat

pies & tarts

Banana Pistachio Pie

¾ cup cinnamon graham cracker crumbs
2 tablespoons reduced-fat margarine, melted
2 packages (4-serving size each) sugar-free fat-free
 pistachio instant pudding and pie filling mix
2½ cups fat-free (skim) milk
1 large ripe banana, sliced
¼ teaspoon ground cinnamon
1 cup thawed frozen reduced-fat whipped topping
 Additional thawed frozen reduced-fat whipped
 topping (optional)

1. Combine graham cracker crumbs and margarine in small bowl; mix until crumbly. Press crumb mixture onto bottom of 9-inch pie plate.

2. Prepare pudding mix according to package directions for pie, using 2½ cups milk. Gently stir in banana and cinnamon; fold in 1 cup whipped topping. Pour into prepared crust. Refrigerate at least 1 hour. Top with additional whipped topping before serving, if desired. *Makes 8 servings*

Nutrients per Serving (1 slice pie):
Calories: 143, **Calories from Fat:** 24%, **Total Fat:** 4g,
Saturated Fat: 1g, **Cholesterol:** 2mg, **Sodium:** 450mg,
Carbohydrate: 22g, **Dietary Fiber:** 1g, **Protein:** 3g

Dietary Exchanges: 1½ Starch, 1 Fat

Banana Pistachio Pie

No-Bake Coconut Cream Pie

2 tablespoons water
1 envelope (¼ ounce) unflavored gelatin
1 can (about 14 ounces) light coconut milk
1 package (8 ounces) fat-free cream cheese
9 packets sugar substitute, divided
2 teaspoons vanilla
1 teaspoon coconut extract
1 low-fat graham cracker pie crust
¼ cup unsweetened grated coconut, toasted*

*To toast coconut, spread in even layer on baking pan. Bake in preheated 350°F oven 5 to 7 minutes, stirring occasionally, until golden brown.

1. Place water in small microwavable bowl. Sprinkle gelatin over water; let stand 1 minute. Microwave on HIGH 20 seconds or until gelatin is completely dissolved.

2. Combine coconut milk, cream cheese, 8 packets sugar substitute, vanilla, coconut extract and gelatin mixture in blender. Cover; process until smooth. Pour mixture into prepared crust; cover and chill 4 hours or until firm.

3. Toss coconut with remaining packet sugar substitute; sprinkle over pie. Cut into 12 slices; serve immediately.

Makes 12 servings

Nutrients per Serving (1 slice pie):
Calories: 118, **Calories from Fat:** 41%, **Total Fat:** 5g,
Saturated Fat: 3g, **Cholesterol:** 2mg, **Sodium:** 175mg,
Carbohydrate: 13g, **Dietary Fiber:** <1g, **Protein:** 4g

Dietary Exchanges: 1 Starch, 1 Fat

No-Bake Coconut Cream Pie

Fresh Strawberry Cream Pie

1 quart fresh medium strawberries
1 tablespoon EQUAL® SPOONFUL*
   Pastry for single-crust 9-inch pie, baked
1 package (8 ounces) reduced-fat cream cheese,
   softened
⅓ cup vanilla-flavored light nonfat yogurt
¼ cup EQUAL® SPOONFUL**
1 tablespoon lemon juice

*You may substitute 1½ packets EQUAL® sweetener.

**You may substitute 6 packets EQUAL® sweetener.

• Remove stems from several strawberries and slice to make 1 cup. Toss with 1 tablespoon Equal® Spoonful. Spread on bottom of baked pie shell.

• Beat cream cheese, yogurt, ¼ cup Equal® Spoonful and 1 tablespoon lemon juice until smooth and fluffy. Spread over sliced strawberries in pie shell. Remove stems from all but 1 large strawberry. Cut berries lengthwise in half. Place, cut side down, over cream cheese mixture, around outer edge of pie crust, with pointed end of berries facing center of pie. Make several thin slits in last whole berry, starting near top and going toward pointed end. Press gently with fingers to form "fan." Place on center of pie.

• Refrigerate pie at least 4 hours before serving.

Makes 8 servings

Nutrients per Serving (1 slice pie):
Calories: 185, **Calories from Fat:** 44%, **Total Fat:** 9g,
Saturated Fat: 6g, **Cholesterol:** 13mg, **Sodium:** 144mg,
Carbohydrate: 13g, **Dietary Fiber:** 1g, **Protein:** 4g

Dietary Exchanges: ½ Starch, ½ Fruit, 2 Fat

Triple Berry Tart

> 1 unbaked (9-inch) refrigerated pie crust
> ¼ cup raspberry fruit spread
> 1½ cups thawed frozen fat-free whipped topping
> 3 ounces reduced-fat cream cheese, softened
> 1½ cups strawberry halves or quarters, hulled
> ½ cup fresh raspberries
> 1⅓ cups fresh or thawed frozen blueberries
> 1 tablespoon powdered sugar

1. Preheat oven to 450°F.

2. Unroll pie crust on large nonstick baking sheet; prick with fork. Bake 8 minutes or until lightly browned. Remove to wire rack; cool completely.

3. Place fruit spread in small microwavable bowl; microwave on HIGH 15 seconds or until slightly melted. Spread evenly over pie crust, leaving ½-inch edge.

4. Beat whipped topping with cream cheese in medium bowl with electric mixer at medium speed until well blended and smooth. Spoon whipped topping mixture evenly over fruit spread. Using back of spoon, smooth whipped topping layer.

5. Arrange berries on top of whipped topping layer. Sprinkle with powdered sugar.   *Makes 8 servings*

Prep Time: 13 minutes

Nutrients per Serving (1 tart wedge):
Calories: 180, **Calories from Fat:** 37%, **Total Fat:** 7g,
Saturated Fat: 2g, **Cholesterol:** 6mg, **Sodium:** 143mg,
Carbohydrate: 26g, **Dietary Fiber:** 2g, **Protein:** 2g

Dietary Exchanges: 1 Starch, ½ Fruit, 1½ Fat

Lemon Meringue Pie

Pastry for single-crust 9-inch pie
2¼ cups water
½ cup fresh lemon juice or frozen lemon juice
  concentrate*
½ cup cornstarch
2 eggs
2 egg whites
1½ teaspoons grated lemon peel
1½ cups EQUAL® SPOONFUL**
2 tablespoons stick butter or margarine
1 to 2 drops yellow food coloring (optional)
3 egg whites
¼ teaspoon cream of tartar
⅔ cup EQUAL® SPOONFUL***

Such as Minute Maid® Premium Lemon Juice (frozen) 100% Pure Lemon Juice from Concentrate

**May substitute 36 packets EQUAL® sweetener.*

***May substitute 16 packets EQUAL® sweetener.*

• Roll pastry on lightly floured surface into circle 1 inch larger than inverted 9-inch pie pan. Ease pastry into pan; trim and flute edge. Pierce bottom and side of pastry with fork. Bake in preheated 425°F oven 10 to 12 minutes or until pastry is golden. Cool on wire rack.

• Combine water, lemon juice and cornstarch in medium saucepan. Bring to a boil over medium-high heat, stirring constantly; boil and stir 1 minute. Beat eggs, 2 egg whites and lemon peel in medium bowl. Mix in 1½ cups Equal® Spoonful. Stir about half of hot cornstarch mixture into egg mixture.

• Return all to saucepan. Cook and stir over low heat 1 minute. Remove from heat; stir in butter until melted. Stir in food coloring, if desired. Pour mixture into baked pie shell.

continued on page 262

Lemon Meringue Pie

Lemon Meringue Pie, continued

• Beat 3 egg whites in medium bowl until foamy. Add cream of tartar and beat to soft peaks. Gradually beat in ⅔ cup Equal® Spoonful, beating to stiff peaks. Spread meringue over hot lemon filling, carefully sealing to edge of crust to prevent shrinking or weeping.

• Bake pie in 425°F oven about 5 minutes or until meringue is lightly browned. Cool completely on wire rack before cutting.

Makes 8 servings

Nutrients per Serving (1 slice pie [⅛ of total recipe]):
Calories: 233, **Calories from Fat:** 47%, **Total Fat:** 12g,
Saturated Fat: 4g, **Cholesterol:** 61mg, **Sodium:** 197mg,
Carbohydrate: 25g, **Dietary Fiber:** 1g, **Protein:** 6g

Dietary Exchanges: 1½ Starch, 2½ Fat

Peppermint Ice Cream Pie

4 cups sugar-free vanilla ice cream
6 sugar-free peppermint candies
1 reduced-fat graham cracker pie crust
¼ cup sugar-free chocolate syrup
Additional sugar-free peppermint candies (optional)

1. Scoop ice cream into medium bowl; let stand at room temperature 5 minutes or until softened, stirring occasionally. Place 6 candies in heavy-duty food storage bag; coarsely crush. Stir candy into ice cream; spread evenly in pie crust.

2. Cover and freeze at least 4 hours or overnight. Cut pie into 12 slices. Transfer to serving plates; drizzle with chocolate syrup. Garnish with additional candies. *Makes 12 servings*

Nutrients per Serving (1 slice pie):
Calories: 147, **Calories from Fat:** 22%, **Total Fat:** 4g,
Saturated Fat: 1g, **Cholesterol:** 0mg, **Sodium:** 134mg,
Carbohydrate: 26g, **Dietary Fiber:** 1g, **Protein:** 3g

Dietary Exchanges: 1½ Starch, ½ Fat

Lattice-Topped Deep-Dish Cherry Pie

2 cans (about 14 ounces each) pitted red tart cherries
    in water
½ cup granular sucralose-based sugar substitute
3 tablespoons quick-cooking tapioca
¼ teaspoon almond extract
¾ cup all-purpose flour
¼ teaspoon salt
3 tablespoons shortening
2 to 3 tablespoons cold water

1. Preheat oven to 375°F. Drain 1 can of cherries. Combine drained cherries, can of cherries with liquid, sugar substitute, tapioca and almond extract in large bowl; set aside.

2. Combine flour and salt in small bowl. Cut in shortening until mixture resembles fine crumbs. Add water, 1 tablespoon at a time, stirring just until dough is moistened. Form dough into ball. Roll dough into 9×8-inch rectangle on lightly floured surface. Cut into 9 (8×1-inch) strips.

3. Spoon cherry mixture into 13×9-inch baking dish. Place 4 pastry strips horizontally over cherry mixture. Weave remaining 5 pastry strips vertically across horizontal strips. Pinch strips at ends to seal. Bake 40 to 50 minutes or until filling is bubbling and pastry is lightly browned. Remove to wire rack; cool slightly. To serve, spoon into bowls.

Makes 9 servings

Prep Time: 15 minutes
Bake Time: 40 to 50 minutes

Nutrients per Serving (⅔ cup pie):
Calories: 126, **Calories from Fat:** 29%, **Total Fat:** 4g,
Saturated Fat: 1g, **Cholesterol:** 0mg, **Sodium:** 72mg,
Carbohydrate: 21g, **Dietary Fiber:** 1g, **Protein:** 2g

Dietary Exchanges: ½ Starch, 1 Fruit, 1 Fat

no-bake desserts

Peach Tapioca

   2 cups reduced-fat (2%) milk
   1 egg, lightly beaten
   3 tablespoons quick-cooking tapioca
1½ cups coarsely chopped peeled peaches*
   3 tablespoons no-sugar-added apricot spread
   1 teaspoon vanilla

*If fresh peaches are not in season, use frozen peaches and add 1 to 2 packets sugar substitute or equivalent of 4 teaspoons sugar to the milk mixture.

1. Combine milk, egg and tapioca in 1½-quart saucepan; let stand 5 minutes. Stir in peaches and apricot spread.

2. Cook and stir over medium heat until mixture comes to a boil; cook 1 minute more. Remove from heat and stir in vanilla.

3. Cool slightly; stir. Place plastic wrap directly on surface of pudding; chill. *Makes 4 servings*

Note: To quickly peel whole peaches, first plunge them into boiling water for about 1 minute.

Nutrients per Serving (¼ of total recipe):
Calories: 155, **Calories from Fat:** 21%, **Total Fat:** 4g,
Saturated Fat: 2g, **Cholesterol:** 62mg, **Sodium:** 92mg,
Carbohydrate: 25g, **Dietary Fiber:** 1g, **Protein:** 6g

Dietary Exchanges: 1½ Fruit, ½ Milk, ½ Fat

Blackberry Sorbet

**1 (8-fluid-ounce) can chilled Vanilla GLUCERNA®
   Shake**
1 cup frozen whole blackberries, unsweetened
½ teaspoon ground cinnamon
¼ teaspoon ground nutmeg
   Sugar substitute to taste

1. Combine all ingredients in blender. Blend until thick.

2. Serve immediately or freeze 10 to 15 minutes.

Makes 2 servings

Nutrients per Serving (¾ cup sorbet):
Calories: 161, **Calories from Fat:** 31%, **Total Fat:** 6g,
Saturated Fat: 1g, **Cholesterol:** 1mg, **Sodium:** 106mg,
Carbohydrate: 23g, **Dietary Fiber:** 5g, **Protein:** 6g

Dietary Exchanges: 1 Starch, ½ Fruit, 1 Fat

tip

Blackberries are packed with antioxidants, the
substances that help fight cancer and heart disease.
This sorbet is a great way to indulge your sweet tooth
without sacrificing any health benefits!

Blackberry Sorbet

Choco-Cherry Chill

1 can (about 14 ounces) tart cherries packed in water, undrained
1½ cups frozen pitted unsweetened dark Bing cherries
1 cup fat-free half-and-half
½ cup reduced-calorie chocolate syrup
1 teaspoon vanilla
Mint sprigs (optional)
Additional frozen pitted unsweetened dark Bing cherries, thawed (optional)

1. Place tart cherries with liquid, frozen Bing cherries, half-and-half and chocolate syrup in blender. Cover and process on HIGH until very smooth.

2. Add vanilla extract; blend until smooth, stop and scrape sides of blender as needed. Freeze cherry mixture in ice cream maker, according to manufacturer's instructions.

3. For best flavor, let stand 15 minutes at room temperature before serving. Garnish each serving with a mint sprig and a thawed Bing cherry. *Makes 8 servings*

Nutrients per Serving (½ cup dessert):
Calories: 62, **Calories from Fat:** 2%, **Total Fat:** <1g,
Saturated Fat: <1g, **Cholesterol:** 4mg, **Sodium:** 41mg,
Carbohydrate: 14g, **Dietary Fiber:** 1g, **Protein:** 2g

Dietary Exchanges: 1 Fruit

Honey Granola with Yogurt

½ cup uncooked old-fashioned oats
¼ cup sliced almonds
2 tablespoons toasted wheat germ
1 tablespoon orange juice
1 tablespoon honey
½ teaspoon ground cinnamon
1½ cups whole strawberries
4 containers (6 ounces each) plain fat-free yogurt
1 teaspoon vanilla

1. Preheat oven to 325°F. Lightly spray 8-inch square baking pan with nonstick cooking spray; set aside.

2. Combine oats, almonds and wheat germ in small bowl. Combine orange juice, honey and cinnamon in another small bowl. Add juice mixture to oat mixture; mix well. Spread mixture evenly into prepared pan. Bake 20 to 25 minutes or until toasted, stirring twice during baking. Transfer mixture to sheet of foil to cool completely.

3. Cut 3 strawberries in half for garnish. Slice remaining strawberries. Combine yogurt and vanilla in medium bowl. Layer yogurt mixture, granola and sliced strawberries in 6 dessert dishes. Garnish with strawberry halves.

Makes 6 servings

Prep Time: 10 minutes
Bake Time: 20 to 25 minutes

Nutrients per Serving (about ½ cup yogurt mixture with ¼ cup strawberries and 2 rounded tablespoonfuls granola):
Calories: 154, **Calories from Fat:** 21%, **Total Fat:** 4g,
Saturated Fat: <1g, **Cholesterol:** 2mg, **Sodium:** 89mg,
Carbohydrate: 22g, **Dietary Fiber:** 2g, **Protein:** 9g

Dietary Exchanges: ½ Starch, ½ Fruit, ½ Milk, ½ Lean Meat, ½ Fat

Tempting Chocolate Mousse

1 envelope unflavored gelatin
2½ cups nonfat milk
¼ cup HERSHEY'S Cocoa or HERSHEY'S SPECIAL DARK™ Cocoa
1 tablespoon cornstarch
1 egg yolk
1 teaspoon vanilla extract
Granulated sugar substitute to equal 8 teaspoons sugar
1 cup prepared sugar-free whipped topping*

*Prepare 1 envelope (1 ounce) sugar-free dry whipped topping mix with ½ cup very cold water according to package directions. (This makes about 2 cups topping; use 1 cup topping for mousse. Reserve remainder for garnish, if desired.)

1. Sprinkle gelatin over milk in medium saucepan; let stand 5 minutes to soften. Stir in cocoa, cornstarch and egg yolk; cook over medium heat, stirring constantly with whisk, until mixture comes to a boil. Reduce heat to low; cook, about 1 minute, stirring constantly, until mixture thickens slightly.

2. Remove from heat; cool to lukewarm. Stir in vanilla and sugar substitute. Pour mixture into medium bowl. Refrigerate about 45 minutes, stirring occasionally until thickened.

3. Fold 1 cup prepared whipped topping into chocolate mixture. Spoon into 6 individual dessert dishes. Cover; refrigerate until firm. Garnish with remaining whipped topping, if desired. *Makes 6 servings*

Nutrients per Serving (⅙ of total recipe [with whipped topping garnish]):
Calories: 95, **Calories from Fat:** 28%, **Total Fat:** 3g,
Saturated Fat: 1g, **Cholesterol:** 35mg, **Sodium:** 86mg,
Carbohydrate: 11g, **Dietary Fiber:** 1g, **Protein:** 6g

Dietary Exchanges: ½ Starch, ½ Milk, ½ Fat

Dreamy Orange Cheesecake Dip

1 package (8 ounces) reduced-fat cream cheese, softened
½ cup orange marmalade
½ teaspoon vanilla
Grated orange peel (optional)
Mint leaves (optional)
2 cups whole strawberries
2 cups cantaloupe chunks
2 cups apple slices

1. Combine cream cheese, marmalade and vanilla in small bowl; mix well. Garnish with orange peel and mint leaves.

2. Serve with strawberries, cantaloupe chunks and apple slices for dipping. *Makes 12 servings*

Note: Dip can be prepared ahead of time. Store, covered, in refrigerator for up to 2 days.

Nutrients per Serving (2 tablespoons dip with ½ cup fruit):
Calories: 102, **Calories from Fat:** 29%, **Total Fat:** 4g,
Saturated Fat: 2g, **Cholesterol:** 7mg, **Sodium:** 111mg,
Carbohydrate: 18g, **Dietary Fiber:** 2g, **Protein:** 3g

Dietary Exchanges: 1 Fruit, ½ Lean Meat, ½ Fat

Ricotta Cheese and Blueberry Parfaits

1 cup whole milk ricotta cheese
1 tablespoon powdered sugar
Grated peel of 1 lemon
1½ cups fresh blueberries

1. Combine ricotta cheese, sugar and lemon peel in medium bowl; mix well.

2. Place 3 tablespoons blueberries in each of 4 parfait glasses. Add ¼ cup ricotta cheese mixture; top with another 3 tablespoons blueberries. *Makes 4 servings*

Nutrients per Serving (⅔ cup parfait):
Calories: 145, **Calories from Fat:** 49%, **Total Fat:** 8g,
Saturated Fat: 5g, **Cholesterol:** 31mg, **Sodium:** 55mg,
Carbohydrate: 12g, **Dietary Fiber:** 2g, **Protein:** 7g

Dietary Exchanges: 1 Fruit, 1 Lean Meat, 1 Fat

acknowledgments

The publisher would like to thank the companies and organizations listed below for the use of their recipes and photographs in this publication.

Almond Board of California

Cabot® Creamery Cooperative

Del Monte Corporation

Dole Food Company, Inc.

Equal® sweetener

Florida Department of Agriculture and Consumer Services, Bureau of Seafood and Aquaculture

Glucerna® is a registered trademark of Ross Products Division of Abbott Laboratories

Guiltless Gourmet®

The Hershey Company

MASTERFOODS USA

Minnesota Cultivated Wild Rice Council

Mrs. Dash®

National Honey Board

National Watermelon Promotion Board

NatraTaste® is a registered trademark of Stadt Holding Corporation

Wheat Foods Council

index

index

index

286

metric conversion chart

VOLUME MEASUREMENTS (dry)

$\frac{1}{8}$ teaspoon = 0.5 mL
$\frac{1}{4}$ teaspoon = 1 mL
$\frac{1}{2}$ teaspoon = 2 mL
$\frac{3}{4}$ teaspoon = 4 mL
1 teaspoon = 5 mL
1 tablespoon = 15 mL
2 tablespoons = 30 mL
$\frac{1}{4}$ cup = 60 mL
$\frac{1}{3}$ cup = 75 mL
$\frac{1}{2}$ cup = 125 mL
$\frac{2}{3}$ cup = 150 mL
$\frac{3}{4}$ cup = 175 mL
1 cup = 250 mL
2 cups = 1 pint = 500 mL
3 cups = 750 mL
4 cups = 1 quart = 1 L

VOLUME MEASUREMENTS (fluid)

1 fluid ounce (2 tablespoons) = 30 mL
4 fluid ounces ($\frac{1}{2}$ cup) = 125 mL
8 fluid ounces (1 cup) = 250 mL
12 fluid ounces (1$\frac{1}{2}$ cups) = 375 mL
16 fluid ounces (2 cups) = 500 mL

WEIGHTS (mass)

$\frac{1}{2}$ ounce = 15 g
1 ounce = 30 g
3 ounces = 90 g
4 ounces = 120 g
8 ounces = 225 g
10 ounces = 285 g
12 ounces = 360 g
16 ounces = 1 pound = 450 g

DIMENSIONS

$\frac{1}{16}$ inch = 2 mm
$\frac{1}{8}$ inch = 3 mm
$\frac{1}{4}$ inch = 6 mm
$\frac{1}{2}$ inch = 1.5 cm
$\frac{3}{4}$ inch = 2 cm
1 inch = 2.5 cm

OVEN TEMPERATURES

250°F = 120°C
275°F = 140°C
300°F = 150°C
325°F = 160°C
350°F = 180°C
375°F = 190°C
400°F = 200°C
425°F = 220°C
450°F = 230°C

BAKING PAN SIZES

Utensil	Size in Inches/Quarts	Metric Volume	Size in Centimeters
Baking or Cake Pan (square or rectangular)	8×8×2	2 L	20×20×5
	9×9×2	2.5 L	23×23×5
	12×8×2	3 L	30×20×5
	13×9×2	3.5 L	33×23×5
Loaf Pan	8×4×3	1.5 L	20×10×7
	9×5×3	2 L	23×13×7
Round Layer Cake Pan	8×1½	1.2 L	20×4
	9×1½	1.5 L	23×4
Pie Plate	8×1¼	750 mL	20×3
	9×1¼	1 L	23×3
Baking Dish or Casserole	1 quart	1 L	—
	1½ quart	1.5 L	—
	2 quart	2 L	—